FDR: ARCHITECT OF AN ERA

A formal portrait, 1939

REXFORD G. TUGWELL

F D R:

ARCHITECT

OF AN ERA

The Macmillan Company, New York

We gratefully acknowledge the following for granting permission to include excerpts of their work in this book:

Duell, Sloan & Pearce, Inc., for *FDR, His Personal Letters* by Elliott Roosevelt. Copyright 1947 by Elliott Roosevelt.

Random House, Inc., for *The Public Papers and Addresses of Franklin D. Roosevelt* by Samuel I. Rosenman.

Harper & Row, Publishers, for *Roosevelt and Hopkins* by Robert E. Sherwood. Copyright 1948 by Robert E. Sherwood.

Doubleday & Company, Inc., for *The Democratic Roosevelt* by Rexford Guy Tugwell. Copyright © 1957 by Rexford Guy Tugwell.

Eleanor Harris for "I Remember Hyde Park" by Eleanor Roosevelt, with Eleanor Harris, which appeared in the February, 1963, issue of *McCall's*.

Samuel I. Rosenman and the Franklin D. Roosevelt Estate for *The Public Papers and Addresses of Franklin D. Roosevelt* by Samuel I. Rosenman.

Illustrations

Introduction

DURING Franklin Delano Roosevelt's administrations the government of the United States began making sure that no one would go hungry or cold, and that everyone would have a decent place to live. This undertaking gave "ordinary" people a sense of security they never had before: a formerly hostile world suddenly became more friendly. This task was not completed at once; time was needed. But beginnings were made, and there were sharp changes from older, careless ways. Only the wealthy had been free of the fear of want until then. This one endeavor was the furthest advance toward equality ever made in this country, and equality had always been a very proud claim among Americans.

Roosevelt spoke of this as *economic* democracy, and said that it gave *political* democracy real meaning. When people could not find jobs, were too old to work, or were disabled, their government would help them. Widows left destitute, and children without fathers, would be supported. Yet they would not be charity cases, either. What came to them would come as their right.

Such risks, Roosevelt said, could easily be met out of the surplus wealth created by our amazing industrial program. We had become the richest country in the world. Yet starvation and cold and homelessness afflicted one-third of our people. How could such neglect be explained or justified? The President put it this way, in 1936:

> It will take courage to let our minds be bold and find the ways to meet the needs of the nation. But for our party now as always, the counsel of courage is the counsel of wisdom.

Here is one-third of a nation ill-nourished, ill-clad, ill-housed
—now!

Here are thousands upon thousands of farmers wondering
whether next year's prices will meet their mortgage interest—
now!

Here are thousands upon thousands of men and women laboring for long hours in factories for inadequate pay—now!

Here are thousands upon thousands of children who should
be at school, working in mines and mills—now!

Here are strikes more far reaching than any we have known
costing millions of dollars—now!

Here are Spring floods threatening to roll again down our river
valleys—now!

Here is the dust bowl beginning to blow again—now!

If we would keep faith with those who had faith in us, if we
would make democracy succeed, I say we must act—now!

Papers, 1937, 121.

It was indeed hard to explain, but for a people so accustomed to self-reliance, it was even harder to accept the
new way. There were many who simply would not or could
not do it. Even the argument furnished by the Great Depression was not impressive enough.

But when after several years of economic paralysis, thirteen
million of the nation's workers were still unemployed, and
fifty million people were in distress, it was obvious the federal
government had to intervene. Local and state governments
had simply run out of funds.

When he became President, Roosevelt met this terrible
emergency by creating and putting into operation a vast organization for meeting it. The Depression was no less a revolution for being a peaceful one. There were no violent mobs;
only a terrible decline into hopelessness. But everyone knew
that the limit had been reached and that something must be
done. Some Congressmen accepted the Roosevelt remedies
with misgivings; but those who objected had no other solu-
tions to offer, and so in the end he prevailed.

He began, as he had to, with emergency measures, bringing the whole federal government into the fight. But, when things were a little better, he went on to the more permanent remedy of a system of social security. He conceived this not only as a humane measure but as one that would prevent in the future such economic ordeals as the nation was then passing through.

He was right. When the social security system was operative, it was so universally approved that not even those who had opposed it hotly when it was first proposed dared suggest giving it up.

Economic sinking spells since Roosevelt's time have been far milder than the old ones. There has been no more paralysis such as there had been in the early thirties. It has gradually come to be understood that there never will be. Something was done that was beneficial to the economy as well as to those who were helped.

This would have been a notable enough accomplishment for one man; as a contribution to democracy it ranked with Jackson's universal suffrage and with Lincoln's emancipation of the slaves. But there was more. For presently, as the struggle for economic recovery and reform was being won, it began to be understood that a new and dangerous force had arisen in the world. It was claimed that democracy was a failure, that equality was nonsense, and that power must be entrusted to those who were competent to grasp and use it. These were totalitarian ideas; their advocates were Hitler and Mussolini.

Totalitarianism itself was not new; it resembled the "divine right" that kings and emperors had once claimed. But it seemed new because the dictators—in Italy, Germany, and Japan—did not inherit their positions but were demagogues who were lifted into power by their distressed people because they offered security in exchange for freedom. People weary after the First World War and worn out with the struggle for a bare living accepted the offer. Hitler became the German Chancellor in the same year that Roosevelt became President of the United States. He and his totalitarian allies were aggressive. They meant to conquer the world and to extinguish the decadent governments opposed to them. It was clear that their challenge had to be met. Roosevelt spoke of the differences between dictatorship and democracies in his Annual Message in 1939:

A dictatorship may command the full strength of a regimented nation. But the united strength of a democratic nation can be mustered only when its people, educated by modern standards to know what is going on and where they are going, have conviction that they are receiving as large a share of opportunity for development, as large a share of material success and of human dignity as they have a right to receive.

Papers, 1939, 5.

It was Roosevelt who persuaded Americans to support the European people who were attacked by Hitler and Mussolini; and it was he who accepted the necessity for the defeat of Japanese aggressors in the Pacific. There followed the mightiest military effort ever organized by the United States, far greater than that undertaken in the First World War. And it succeeded.

After the years of struggle, as victory was within sight, Roosevelt turned his mind to the establishment of world security, as he had before to American social security. It was not enough to defeat the enemy; a way must be found to prevent future wars, to make peace permanent, to give people the relief from dangers always hanging over them. Roosevelt spoke of these aims in a 1939 Armistice Day address at Virginia Military Institute:

The only object of arms is to bring about a condition in which quiet peace under liberty can endure. In this season we have been used to celebrating the Armistice of the World War. Now we need a new and better peace: a peace which shall cause men at length to lay down weapons of hatred . . . and to forego purposeless ambitions which have created fear. . . . We seek a language in which neighbor can talk to neighbor; in which men can talk to men; and by which the common and homely and human instincts which are found everywhere may reach expression. . . .

I have sought and I still seek, in all simplicity to find the road to this peace. It must be the goal not only of men trained to arms, but of all of us everywhere. . . .

Papers, 1939.

The United Nations was Roosevelt's creation more than any one's else—unless it was his wife Eleanor's. She had worked to further his career, to turn it in the directions it had taken, to make the underprivileged secure and—now—to create a workable United Nations. It was the last major project of both their lives.

This book is one sort of record. It is meant to describe the transformations that took place during the Roosevelt years, to speak of his education in politics, and to show how he used its arts to achieve the well-being of the nation, then peace. His intention was to start something that would never end. This record is meant to show what that was, and how it was brought about.

R. G. Tugwell
Southern Illinois University

The Roosevelt Chronology

1828   Birth of James, Franklin's father.

1854   Birth of Sara Delano, Franklin's mother.

1882   Birth of Franklin at Springwood in Hyde Park Township of Dutchess County, New York.

1884   Birth of Anna Eleanor Roosevelt on a nearby estate.

1885–90 Franklin is tutored at home and goes on journeys abroad with parents.

1891   First experience of school at Bad Nauheim for six weeks.

1896   After more tutoring and travel, is entered at Groton School.

1897   Establishes himself at Groton with some difficulty.

1898   Still at Groton, watches Theodore Roosevelt's campaign for governor, his father James having bolted the Democratic party to support the Republican candidate Roosevelt.

1899   Is taken to Theodore Roosevelt's inauguration in Albany.

1900   Enters Harvard; tries for athletic teams but has no success; father dies.

1901   Tours Europe with mother; begins to report for the *Crimson;* fails of election to Porcellian; is chosen for Fly Club.

1902   Protests British treatment of Boers; works hard at reporting; very busy with Cambridge society.

1903   Elected president of the *Crimson*; becomes engaged to

Eleanor, a distant cousin; substantially finishes college course with average grades.

1904   An extra year at Harvard; studies economics, political science, and history. Takes a winter trip to the Caribbean and Panama. Graduates in spring. Enters Columbia University School of Law in fall.

1905   Goes to Theodore Roosevelt's inauguration as President. Is married to Eleanor and they have a long honeymoon in Europe.

1906   Daughter, Anna Eleanor, is born.

1907   Admitted to the Bar; becomes clerk in the firm of Carter, Ledyard and Milburn. Son, James, is born. Begins to buy acreage of his own at Hyde Park for farming and forestry experiments.

1908   Predicts casually to fellow clerks that he will be President and tells how he will manage it.

1909   Son, first Franklin Delano, Jr., is born in March and dies in November.

1910   Nominated for state senator by Dutchess County Democrats and elected. Son, Elliott, is born.

1911   Involves himself in protest against election of Sheehan for senator, thus incurring Tammany enmity but making a name for himself. Is spotted by Louis McHenry Howe, Albany newsman, as likely to go far politically. Gradually becomes a ticketed Progressive. Decides to support Woodrow Wilson as a way of entering national politics and escaping Tammany wrath.

1912   Organizes Wilson's support in New York; goes to Baltimore convention; is re-elected in spite of sickness during campaign, with Howe taking charge.

1913   Is appointed Assistant Secretary of the Navy; resigns as state senator and escapes from Tammany.

1914   Is unsuccessful candidate for governorship nomination against Gerard and learns more about Tammany power. Second Franklin Delano, Jr., is born.

1914–17 Supervises labor in Navy yards; handles Navy contracts; comes under admirals' influence and is known as a big-Navy man. Is separated in policy from Daniels concerning preparedness. Interested in Caribbean, especially Haiti and Marines; also visits Cuba and Santo Domingo. Irritated with Wilson and Daniels, who are not sufficiently martial to suit him. Develops social life in Washington; makes many friends among the diplomatic set. Gradually makes peace with Tammany and is urged to run for governor in 1916 but declines.

1916 Last child, John Aspinwall, is born.

1918 Wilson suggests that he run for governor, but he decides on war service. Goes abroad to see war after many attempts and tries to become officer on his return but is too late.

1919 Goes abroad to visit Peace Conference and settle Navy affairs. Returns on the *George Washington* with Wilson and becomes a convert to peace organization.

1920 Is nominated for the Vice-Presidency (with James M. Cox, the Democrats intending his selection to soften the slight to Wilson of Cox's nomination; actually Wilson did not approve); campaigns widely and, although the contest is lost, builds up party acquaintance all over the country. Becomes vice-president of the Fidelity and Deposit Company of Maryland with office in Wall Street. Also practices law with Emmet and Marvin.

1921 Stricken with poliomyelitis.

1922–24 Works at convalescence; tries various doctors, places, and cures. Goes to Florida Keys for winter exercise in warm water. Eleanor works with Howe to encourage Franklin and discovers her own personality. Warm Springs is found and seems to be a place where exercise in the pool will assist in recovering the use of his lower body. Participates in Smith attempt to gain nomination for Presidency. Makes "Happy Warrior" speech. Has Smith and Davis at Hyde Park for reconciliation. Eleanor becomes politically active.

1924   Forms law partnership with D. B. O'Connor.

1924–28 Puts Smith in nomination at Houston convention, making second "Happy Warrior" speech. After reluctant evasions, feels forced to take nomination for governorship and is elected by narrow majority even though Smith is defeated for the Presidency.

1928–30 Develops independence in the governorship which involves coolness in relations with Smith.

1930   Is re-elected by largest majority registered until that time. Becomes Presidential candidate.

1932   Nominated for the Presidency against Hoover and wins election in midst of Depression.

1933   Gives the nation action to combat deepening economic crisis. Eleanor becomes effective collaborator.

1934–36 Very gradual economic recovery and continued experimentation; but gradual erosion of control over the Congress.

1936   Is re-elected in overwhelming victory over Alfred M. Landon.

1936–40 Accelerated loss of power. Disastrous Court fight contributes to fading out of New Deal by strengthening reactionaries. Preparedness becomes chief preoccupation as war breaks out in Europe and line-up against dictators takes place. Tries for conciliation but fails.

1940   Is re-elected by narrowed majority over Wendell Willkie. Makes first decision to proceed with work leading to fission of uranium.

1941   Leads the nation into war against Japan and Germany after the provocation of Pearl Harbor. Luckily, Hitler has attacked Russia and a general nutcracker strategy is possible.

1942   Assumes substantial leadership of Allies. Churchill conforms. War reached crisis as Germany and Japan spread their empires with amazing speed.

1943 War turns toward eventual victory; tremendous war effort in the United States begins to have effect. Franklin becomes strategist-in-chief, communicating with Churchill and Stalin, but always having the last say because of immense U.S. power. January, Casablanca Conference; August, Quebec; November-December, Cairo-Teheran, where Stalin is met face to face for the first time.

1944 Victory approaches, and outlines of organization for peace take shape; Franklin is their sponsor and negotiator. D-Day; invasion of Europe occurs on June 6; after stubborn fighting in Normandy, armies sweep across France. Opens negotiations with Wendell Willkie for new party alignment to unite the nation's progressive forces. Willkie agrees but postpones action until after election. Is re-elected to the Presidency over Thomas E. Dewey. Feels Dewey most unscrupulous of all his opponents, but wins by still narrower majority.

1945 Final conference at Yalta in February gives shape to coming peace. Begins to believe the postwar world may be made secure not only from war but also from want. In his last months he turns again to the progressive agenda for prosperity and fair sharing. Yalta arrangements begin to come apart in the unskillful hands of seconds as San Francisco meeting to establish permanent United Nations approaches. Dies as Germany crumbles and before Japan has finally collapsed, but in the clear prospect of military victory; also before he could carry further his scheme for party realignment; aged sixty-three years, two months.

One-year-old Franklin
with his father,
James Roosevelt

With his father, 1887

YOUNG Franklin spent his first fourteen years—from 1882 to 1896—on a large country place called Springwood, about a hundred miles up the Hudson River from New York City. The estate had nearly everything a boy could want. There was a big home, because his father was wealthy; and it was always comfortable, because his mother was a good manager. There were also devoted servants; fields and woods to play in; and horses, dogs, and all the usual farm animals.

A typical view of his life as a boy is shown in a letter written by Franklin to his aunt when he was nine years old.

MY DEAR AUNT DOE,

We are having a very early Spring and the wild flowers are beginning to come up in the woods. My pony Debby is well and I rode 12 miles today with Papa and we are going to ride to Algonac as we did last Summer. I am to have a little farm and chicken house of my own. . . . Please tell Uncle Will that if has any foreign stamps I should like to have them, as I have begun to make a collection.

Papa is going to buy a cutter that will go by naphtha and we are going to sail in it at Campobello and here. . . .

Your affectionate nephew
FRANKLIN

Letters: Early Years, 18.

Aunt Doe was Mrs. Forbes who lived for many years in Macao, an island off the mainland of China. She was his mother's sister and grew up with his mother at the Delano home, Algonac, across the Hudson. Debby was his first pony.

The cutter turned out to be the fifty-foot *Half Moon,* object of his affection for many years.

The Hudson River, so wide there at Krum Elbow (where Springwood was located) that it seemed like a lake, was just down a slope through meadows, orchards, and woods. And boys, even small ones, always like to be near water. Franklin had the run of the whole place, with a pony to ride whenever he liked.

He had a room of his own where as a small boy he could keep his toys and later could store his collections of stamps, stuffed birds, and minerals. He could read there or entertain his friends. It was even a pleasant place to be sick, although this did not happen often, as is shown in the following letter to his parents, who were in New York:

> Feb. 27, 1892
> HYDE PARK
>
> MY DARLING MUMKIN AND PAP,
>
> Good morning, I hope you have used Pears soap and are flourishing. I am dying of school fever and you will be horrified to hear that my temperature is 150 degrees. But really I have got a "petit rheume" only I am in the hands of the celebrated Dr. Sandoz—He came up to see me this morning & ordered 5 drops of camfer on sugar twice in the morning; a hot toe bag, breakfast in bed and stay home all day tomorrow and today if not clear of the disease. I went to play with E. yesterday and rided over there—Today the whole army of carpenters come to lunch. We got 12 eggs yesterday and there is no clocking hen.
>
> Your affectionate,
> ROOSEVELT DELANO FRANKLIN
>
> P.S. The thermometer went down to 10 last night. High wind all night.

Letters: Early Years.

(The "celebrated Dr. Sandoz" was his governess.

The eggs were from his own chickens. E. was Edmund Rogers, his close friend.)

And the fact is that, sick or well, during those years he was never lonely or unhappy. This was partly because his home was pleasant, but even more because he had an interest in everything around him that made him want to know how it lived or worked. He found the answers to his questions sometimes by reading and experimenting, but more often by exploring and asking questions. His mind sopped up information as a blotter sops up ink. What he learned stayed there too; it was one of his most helpful characteristics. He was active as much as possible:

SPRINGWOOD, 1893

DEAR MAMMY,

I hope you are much better today and that you will be able to go out today . . . Yesterday I worked all morning on joice [joists] for the club house and in the afternoon Edmund and I put two of them up. I dined and supped at Edmund's but Melle. got there at 6.40 so we had not any time to play. Today Edmund is coming to lunch and we will get the other joice up. . . .

With bales of love to everybody,

Your devoted baby,
NILKARF

Letters: Early Years.

(In the collection of *Letters* a note explains that Edmund Rogers recalled the incident of the "joice." The boys were building a small-boat club house, and planned to dam a small stream below the Roosevelt home on which to sail model yachts.)

What made Franklin's life different from that of most boys was that he did belong in a wealthy family and in a neighborhood where the other families were wealthy too. It was a long time before he realized that there was anything unusual about this, and even then he was inclined to accept his good fortune without question.

The Roosevelts were generous and considerate. They may have felt themselves superior, but they never let it be seen.

During the last years of the nineteenth and the first years of the twentieth century wealth was more easily kept after it had been gained than it was after the income tax was enacted by constitutional amendment in 1913. But by that time,

3

Franklin was grown and a member of the New York State Senate. Until then the family fortune made life easy.

Events of great importance, however, were about to occur that would make enormous differences in such family fortunes. These events were to increase the expenditures of the government—and the need for revenues, too. So there would have to be higher taxes. These events were the First World War, and later the Great Depression. Franklin himself would be prominent in these future happenings. He was preparing for this—all unaware—during the years of his boyhood and youth. But in that future time, luxurious living would be less common.

There were friends next door to Springwood—the Rumbolds, who had a daughter, Mary. The Rogers children lived about a mile away. There were three of them. Edmund Rogers was within six months of Franklin's age and was a special friend.

All the houses along the river were surrounded by many acres and to get from one to another was something of a walk. The homes stood far back from the Albany Post Road and long private driveways led to each of them. Hyde Park village was several miles to the north; and Poughkeepsie, a good deal farther to the south, was the only nearby city.

There was a school in Hyde Park; but Franklin never attended it. Wealthy boys got their early education in a different way. They had governesses first and then tutors. Franklin's teachers made a considerable impression on him, and he recalled most of them with affection.

Although he may have missed the playmates he might have had in school, he probably learned a good deal more than he would have in the Hyde Park classrooms. Languages were not taught there; at home he began to learn French and German. He learned something of school life from joining with the Rogers children next door for some of their lessons. This was supplemented by frequent travels with his father and mother—with governess or tutor going along as well. His father was partially retired from business, although he went

4

to an office in New York several times a week. He was fifty-four years old when Franklin was born and was more like a grandfather than a father to the boy. Because of this and because money was plentiful, he took his family abroad several months each year.

MY DEAR EDMUND,

I am writing to you on the *Teutonic*. She is the largest ship I ever saw. She is 582 feet long and 56 feet broad and 39 feet depth of hold. She has almost everything on board; there is a library, a barber shop, lots of baths, and lots of other things where you get quite lost. We are rolling now so I can hardly write. The waves are quite high. When one is sitting down one has to take care one does not slip off. Please write soon. Good bye.

I am your affectionate,
FRANKLIN

P.S. I had a fight with a big boy of eleven because he cheated and I beat him.

Letters: Early Years.

Franklin was hardly more than a boy when his father's health began to be a problem and, as was fashionable for wealthy people then, he went to various resorts to "take the cure." The regimen in these places allowed him to see a good deal of his son. They were very good companions, and when they were in Hyde Park, as well as when they were abroad or at a resort, they spent hours of each day together. Franklin was taken on inspection trips over the farm—nearly four hundred acres—and got to know all about its operations.

The European trips had their own interest, although Franklin would often rather have stayed home where his friends and interests were. But usually he and his tutor were left in some pleasant place where he could find the things to do that a boy especially enjoys. He had lessons every day, he made friends wherever he went, and often organized games and expeditions.

In 1889 the family set out for Europe; when they set sail Franklin was not feeling well, and on the ship it was discovered that he had typhoid fever. He was taken to the Royal

Infirmary in Liverpool when they landed. Recovery was slow and it was thought that Pau, in the south of France, would be good both for him and for his father, who was also ill. In Pau they rode in the country for two hours every morning and quickly recovered. He became so fond of Coquette, the pony he rode, that he grudged the time he had to spent on lessons.

But his German and Swiss teachers were strict, and able, and in later travels that summer, he made good progress. When the family came home to Hyde Park, Mademoiselle Sandoz became his governess for three years and, of all his tutors and governesses, she was recalled most fondly when he was grown.

When he was old enough, he was allowed to go on walking trips by himself. Once he spent some months in a German school, his only experience of formal education until he was sent to Groton, when he was fourteen, in preparation for Harvard.

These trips abroad may not have been exactly what Franklin would have chosen for himself, but for a boy who was to grow up to be President of the United States, they had their own importance. They gave him an awareness of a larger world than that of Dutchess County, New York, where Springwood was located; they taught him that other people and other manners were acceptable and that his own country, although agreeable indeed, was only one of many nations with hopes and ambitions of their own. Such a background helped him to realize that the rest of the world was important to Americans.

These journeys were varied by stays in New York City, although Franklin avoided the city whenever he could. He was a country boy; and the city had few attractions to match those at home. This, too, was something that would characterize him as a man. He was to carry into his work in his own state, and then into his work in Washington, a special love for the countryside. It made him a conservationist when the movement for protection of forests, waters, and wildlife was just

6

Age eleven

getting well under way. And it would make him the kind of President who would always want to do what he could for people who worked on the land. Here is Frank Freidel, one of Roosevelt's biographers, on this subject:

> It was from his father that Franklin absorbed considerable knowledge of the land and its management. His early interest in care of the trees led years later to his own extensive forestry. The dairy cattle and a remaining pair of trotting horses fascinated him, and he shared his father's pride in the memory of Gloster, a champion trotter which James Roosevelt had sold some years before Franklin's birth to Senator Leland Stanford, founder of Stanford University. Later Gloster was killed in a train wreck, but his tail, strangely enough, was presented to Franklin fifty years later, and ultimately it adorned a wardrobe in a corner of the President's bedroom in the White House.

Roosevelt, The Apprenticeship, 23.

It should be recalled that while Franklin was enjoying the privilege of education and travel in such circumstances, all was not well in the United States. Franklin's father, as an investor, was especially interested in railways; and the railways and Wall Street were blamed for the depression of 1893 and the bad years that followed. The farmers felt that they were charged too much by the railroad for getting their crops to market, and they were sure that this was because speculators were making fortunes out of railway securities. The farmers' indignation was responsible for the first severe regulation of business by the government.

This was part of the same movement, headed by William Jennings Bryan, that was responsible for a serious agitation for cheap money. As the West and South were opened up and more land was plowed, there was an immense increase in the crops of corn, wheat, and cotton. It flooded markets; prices fell, and this made it hard for farmers to pay back the loans they had contracted when the prices they received had been high. It was with borrowed capital that most of the new

8

country had been opened up. And the capital had been bor-rowed from the bankers in the East.

"Wall Street" was the symbolic phrase for these creditors. It was against them that much of the resentment of those years was directed. The debtors thought that if they could not get high prices then the government might enlarge the supply of money, thus making it easier to acquire when debts had to be paid. They wanted to go off the "gold standard" (money based solely on the value of gold) and include silver in the medium of exchange. Some even wanted the govern-ment merely to print money without gold or silver as back-ing. These dollars were called greenbacks, and they had been used during the Civil War. Anything would do if it increased the number of dollars and thus lightened the load of debt.

There was bitter division in the nation. It persisted through-out Franklin's boyhood, and his father was one of the severely criticized capitalists.

It was not until Franklin was further along in life, however, and began to study American history that he became aware of all this. He was protected at Hyde Park and on his travels from any hint that there were struggles and disputes over such issues in the outside world. He may well have heard of Bryan and perhaps even of some of the other western agitators; but if he did, it made no impression on him at the time. And when he came to understand that the family fortune was built on railway speculation we do not know.

(2)

WHEN, as an older boy, Franklin wanted ponies he got them, but only after he had promised to look after them himself. When he was still older and wanted an iceboat for winter days on the river, he got that too—after he had demonstrated that he could manage the tricky contraption; iceboats were speedy, and sailing them could be dangerous for anyone heavily bundled up against freezing winds. His father meant him to be responsible, and this was one way of seeing that he would be. He had less trouble about his first sailing craft. This he got when he had learned to swim and so could venture beyond his depth with safety. But there was the same requirement. He must be capable of going through with whatever he undertook.

The family not only possessed the Hyde Park estate and often went abroad, but spent many summers at Campobello, an island off the coast of Canada just over the United States border. The Roosevelts spoke of their home there as a cottage; but actually it was almost as large as the house in Hyde Park. The water around Campobello is the Bay of Fundy. It is cold and deep, and its mighty tides are dangerous. Learning to handle a boat there was something that would have tried the skill of any boy.

Franklin became an expert sailor among the channels and islands; but it was only when he was sixteen that his old twenty-one-foot knockabout was replaced by a genuine fifty-foot deep-sea craft. The *Half Moon* may well have been the most precious possession Franklin ever acquired. Certainly it taught him self-reliance, as well as the many skills necessary to the maintenance and handling of a boat of that size in really perilous waters.

Having possessions of this sort and learning to use and care for them was an important part of his parents' training program for Franklin. He would always have the responsibilities of wealth, and in their view, wealth carried obligations. He must learn to administer it so that it provided the best possible life for all those around him.

The term *noblesse oblige* is as good a one as any to explain the attitude Franklin's parents wanted him to develop. Accepting the obligations of his fortunate position was as much the mark of his later public life as of his boyhood. He felt that the rich should share with the poor, that all should have equal opportunities, and that the government had an obligation to see that the national heritage was made available to everyone equally. This was further than his parents would have gone; and it was certainly an annoyance to many of his wealthy contemporaries. They said he was a traitor to his class. But the course he followed seemed quite natural to him and he never varied from it.

As President, after the Great Depression had struck and suffering was widespread, this attitude of his led to a drastic change in America: one that made an enormous advance toward the equality that the country's Founding Fathers had conceived, but that had been so largely forgotten by their descendants. What others of Franklin's generation and class could not bear was giving up privileges and sharing with others the power they had so long monopolized. It was the boy who had been taught *noblesse oblige* by a wise father and mother who furnished the leadership for the movement known in our history as the New Deal.

Being the only child of parents whose hopes were centered in him was sometimes difficult. He liked to be free, as any boy would; and there were often more interesting activities than the duties he was asked to carry out. But the discipline was so easy and so reasonable that he accepted it without much protest. This was easier for him because he liked to please and because affection was necessary to his happiness. It was a real punishment to see his parents unhappy because of something he had done. He grew up well within the rules of the family and gave promise of turning out as they wanted him to.

As a boy Franklin showed no specialized gifts of any sort. He was not particularly good at arithmetic; he possessed no aptitude for music; he could not draw; and he was no better at writing than he needed to be for ordinary communication. There was no reason to think he would become an engineer, for instance, or a doctor. And this rather pleased his parents. What they wanted for him was a good and decent life of the same sort they were having. They rather hoped he would study law, because then he would be able to look after the family affairs. But they also wanted him to know about farming and forestry, so that he could manage Springwood. He would, his parents hoped, be a country gentleman with some outside interests. He would live quietly and usefully and raise another generation of Roosevelts.

To be a Roosevelt meant something. Franklin's ancestors, Dutch and English, had been in and about New York since before the Revolutionary War. They had been merchants and financiers, growing a little more wealthy with each generation. They were sound and solid citizens. Every once in a while one would be listed as a member of some civic committee, the head of some charitable organization, or the leader in a business or banking enterprise. It was, in short, a substantial, a respectable family.

In the generation of James, Franklin's father, there were two especially prominent branches of the family. Besides the one in Hyde Park on the Hudson, there was one in Oyster Bay on Long Island. The Oyster Bay branch was better known because of Theodore, who was to reach the Presidency while Franklin was at Harvard. But even while Franklin was at Groton, Theodore was a national hero and a hero to Franklin, as can be seen by this letter:

At Hyde Park with his mother, 1898

June 4, 1897
GROTON

DEAR PAPA AND MAMA,

Cousin Theodore came today and wants me to stay with him for July 4th, so I have decided to divide my time at Oyster Bay between him and Cousin Bammie. . . .

After supper tonight Cousin Theodore gave us a splendid talk on his adventures when he was on the Police Board. He kept the whole room in an uproar for over an hour, by telling us killing stories about policemen and their doings in New York. . . .

Letters: Early Years.

Theodore had been Assistant Secretary of the Navy (as Franklin was to become) when the Spanish-American War had begun and had resigned to organize the Rough Riders, a regiment of cavalry that made itself and its commander famous at the Battle of San Juan Hill in Cuba. This was characteristic of Theodore. He was a natural politician; and this meant that he sought publicity, called attention to himself, and repeatedly campaigned for office.

The Oyster Bay and the Hyde Park Roosevelts did not get together very often; but there was no unfriendliness. As Uncle

13

Ted became Governor, and then President, Franklin sometimes visited the executive mansion in Albany and the White House in Washington. James Roosevelt was a prominent Democrat and had taken Franklin with him to the White House even earlier—when Cleveland was President. Franklin's father, as a matter of fact, spent the whole winter of 1887 in Washington in the interest of a business venture. He and other businessmen expected to build a canal from ocean to ocean; and, actually, a bill of incorporation for the Maritime Canal Company of Nicaragua did pass the Congress and was signed by Cleveland.

Nothing came of this venture. Hard times came and capital could not be raised. And, of course, later on the government, not a private company, did build the canal—across Panama, not Nicaragua. Uncle Ted, as President, was to be its promoter. Franklin was only five that winter of 1887, so his memories of Washington must have been dim by the time he was grown. But his mother did record in her diary that "even Franklin knew everybody!" And "everybody" included. President Cleveland.

There is good reason to think that the reserve Franklin learned at home was considerably modified by admiration for the other Roosevelt, who was even then fighting his way into prominence without paying too much attention to the rules for gentlemanly conduct. Matching the achievement of Uncle Ted was certainly one of the compelling motives of his later career. In the end there would turn out to be some remarkable parallels: Both served in the New York State legislature, both became Governor, both were Assistant Secretary of the Navy, and both were elected to the Presidency. Of the two, it is probably Franklin who will be judged the more important force in American history. The later Roosevelt had more serious crises to meet, crises of such magnitude as Uncle Ted could hardly have imagined. If Franklin became the more noted statesman, the circumstances had something to do with it. But he did have the Roosevelt flair, and he made the most of it.

(3)

IT must be said that, as a Groton schoolboy, Franklin showed no promise of future prominence. He was neither very good nor very bad as a scholar; and the same was true of athletics. His worst trouble was that his fond mother had kept him at home too long. He ought to have entered Groton when he was twelve, as his classmates did; instead, he was two years late, and the other boys had already made those friendships that are so close in boarding school. A newcomer had to break into groups already established. He was accepted in time and even became popular; but it was not easy, and he was not good enough at any activity to be encouraged by praise. Characteristically, he made the best of his situation; and his letters home were always cheerful. Here is his first letter from Groton, written when he was fourteen.

DEAR MOMMERR & POPPERR,

I am getting on finely both mentally and physically. I sit next a boy named A. Gracie King at meals, he is from Garrison and knows the Pells and Morgans.

I am still in the 3rd A & I think I am about half way up. I am all right in Latin, Greek, Science and French; a little rusty in Algebra but not more so than the others. I played football today on the 4th twenty-two (7th eleven). . . .

Just got your letter and also one from Mr. Dumper. He is in Mt. Vernon and well. It rained this morning but has stopped now.

We have just had Latin and Algebra, and we study French tonight. We went to Mrs. Peabody's parlor last night for half an hour and played games.

I got the shoes last night with the toothpowder; the shoes are just right.

We are off to dinner now so I cannot write more but I will write you Sunday.

With lots of love,
FDR.

Letters: Early Years.

His late start at Groton was made more difficult because, at fourteen, he was tall and gangly and still sang soprano in the choir. The next year his soprano voice changed to tenor, but this was late. The other boys were ahead of him in physical maturing, and his efforts to keep up with their activities were painful. Changing from being a boy to being a man was even harder in a boarding school where everyone knew everyone else so well. Franklin was terribly conscious of his boyishness and pretended as best he could to be older than he was. This, as we shall see, explains much, even in his later career.

Pleasing others, however, was something he did very well, because he was naturally agreeable and charming. He might have been resentful and withdrawn; but instead he always tried to win approval. What he felt inside was very different from what appeared outside.

He became something of an actor. No one knew what his trials were. And it is hard to say whether this was fortunate for him or otherwise. Troubled boys can often find comfort in a father's counsel, but James was growing old and somewhat distant. Franklin's headmaster was something of a substitute, but mostly he had to act independently. This probably served to toughen him for the hard battles of adult life.

Groton was not an old school. It had been founded only a few years before by Endicott Peabody, an Episcopal clergyman who had a very definite purpose: to train the sons of the better families in America for the responsibilities of life—to make them "Christian gentlemen." It was intended to be the American version of English public schools like Eton and Harrow, so very much admired for having produced the ruling class of an empire. The regimen was austere; discipline was rigorous; and conformity to school standards was enforced. The boys slept in common dormitories, began their days with cold baths, ate very plain fare, were expected to study hard, and were practically forced into competitive games, not only for the body-building, but even more to accustom them to team play, regarded as so important a part of English education. It used to be said that the British Empire was won on the playing fields of Eton. Peabody hoped athletics at Groton would have a similar importance in the growth of the United States.

Some of the sporting events were rather strange.

> March 24, 1897
> GROTON

DEAR PAPA AND MAMA,

Last Monday was a red-letter day for me; in the morning after school we had the III Class High Kick. There were about 15 entries. . . . A tin pan was suspended from the ceiling of the Gym, about 3½ feet from the floor at first. As it rose the contestants dropped out one by one until I found myself one of the only three left. . . . At the next rise in the pan Crocker dropped out and at the next rise Robeson missed the kick three times and I twice. As we were only allowed three tries, Robeson was out of it and at my 3rd kick I just touched the pan which secured 1st prize to me. . . .

At every kick I landed on my neck on the left side so the result is that the whole left side of my body is sore and my left arm is a little swollen.

Letters: Early Years.

But mostly, athletics were of a more normal kind, and two years later, Franklin was made manager of the baseball team.

> Memorial Day, 1899

DEAR MAMA AND PAPA,

This A.M. we had lunch at 12:30 and right after left in barges for the village; we lined up just on the outskirts and marching to the townhall joined the veterans and from there marched to the cemetery. We then had lemonade and oranges in a hut near the cemetery and then marched back to the town. I had a soda and walked right back as the nine had their last practice. I fear the outlook for tomorrow is not very promising; the nine had good capabilities but utterly lacks team-play and snap. . . .

Wednesday [next day]: Well, we were beaten as we expected, 25–6.

Letters: Early Years.

The Groton atmosphere pleased Franklin's parents. They were Episcopalians, too, and they admired everything English. The training they had begun at home, they felt, was being continued at school. And, of course, it was. Franklin accepted the discipline without protest. He did his lessons and passed his tests. He took part in all the activities and did the best he could. He was too tall and gangly for football; but he tried, realizing how much it meant to make a team. He got some approval from his classmates for the effort.

After a year the strangeness wore off. If he was not an outstanding success at anything, he was a good enough Grotonian. The separation from his parents was not much regretted. The school had become the center of his life.

It was the intention of Peabody that Christianity should become a vital part of his pupils' lives. And with Franklin, at least, the intention succeeded. There is reason to think that he found in the heavenly Father not only a substitute for the father he was now separated from but a refuge in the trials of growing up and making his way at Groton. He did not talk much about this. His acceptance was a quiet one, not to be discussed, but it was deeply felt. This, too, was the beginning of a life-long habit. He would always be a practicing Christian, finding comfort in God, and believing that he could always seek divine help.

His Christian feelings showed in tangible ways outside activities at Groton. He was a member of a missionary society whose purpose was to be helpful to those less fortunate. He helped with religious services in isolated country churches and took on the duty of looking after several poor families in the neighborhood.

DEAREST MAMA AND PAPA,

The Missionary Society has appointed Warren Motley and myself as special missionaries to look after Mrs. Freeman, an

FDR (*center*), manager of the baseball team at Groton, 1899–1900

old woman near the school. She is an old colored lady, living all alone, and 84 years old. We payed our first visit to her today, right after church, and talked and gave her the latest news, for nearly an hour. We are to visit her a couple of times a week, see that she has coal, water, etc., feed her hens if they need it, and in case of snow-storm we are to dig her out, and put things in ship shape. It will be very pleasant as she is a dear old thing, and it will be a good occupation for us. . . .

Letters, I, 254.

That the charitable feeling influenced the welfare activities of Franklin's New Deal there can be no doubt. Perhaps he did not discover in Groton that private charity is not enough; but the seed of such a thought may well have been planted during his schoolboy visitations.

Eventually his Groton life began to seem normal. He found it hard to realize that he was about to graduate into the collegiate world of the Harvard Yard. He was now nineteen, six feet three, handsome and energetic. He was still a beanpole, useless in football. And he had not yet discovered that football honors were not the most important ones he could win. He still hoped to fill out and make the Harvard team.

Endicott Peabody remembered him this way in a letter to another Grotonian in 1932:

There has been a good deal written about Franklin Roosevelt when he was a boy at Groton, more than I should have thought justified by the impression that he left at the school. He was a quiet, satisfactory boy of more than ordinary intelligence, taking a good position in his form but not brilliant. Athletically he was too slight for success. We all liked him. So far as I know this is true of the masters and boys alike.

Letters, 34.

It is not certain that the Groton product was quite so admirable as Peabody believed. Franklin and the other private-school graduates were moving into luxurious dormitories at

Harvard (called the "Gold Coast") and forming cliques that effectively shut out those who came from less exclusive schools. They had learned democracy within the Groton group, but they definitely felt that they belonged to an elite. They had learned, perhaps, that they had obligations—but mostly because inferiors had to be looked after.

(4)

FRANKLIN lost his father in his freshman year at Harvard. Apart from the grief he felt because his father and he had been close companions before he had gone to Groton, this made a considerable difference in another way; he was now the only heir to the family fortune, and this involved serious obligations. He was also more than ever the center of his mother's watchful care.

Some of her traits, not so noticeable before his father's death, now showed themselves. She thought it her duty to take charge of his life; and this to her meant close supervision. She moved to Boston where the Roosevelts had many connections, and set out to do her duty.

What a problem this was for Franklin can best be understood by knowing what an imposing and determined matron his mother had become. The family she came from—the Delanos—considered itself to be as important as the Roosevelts. They, too, lived on a Hudson River estate, and Sara as a girl had been taught the importance of her position. She never forgot for a moment that her son came from distinguished stock; she felt that she was responsible for seeing that he developed into a man who accepted properly the responsibilities of his inheritance.

Franklin, who was always anxious to please and to conform in social matters, accepted his mother's attentions in the manner of a dutiful son. Yet he managed to develop a mind of his own about things that seemed to him important. If he had really conformed to his mother's wishes, he would have had no part in public affairs, no general sympathy for the well-being of *all* the people (so different from his family's concern for only those within their small circle of dependents), and no curiosity about the democracy he believed in.

At Harvard in this first year, Franklin maintained an average grade of C. This might seem to show indifference. However, his letters attest to his interest in his studies; but also to the amount of time given to numerous other activities. These accounted for his low grades.

WESTMORLY COURT
September, 1900

DEAREST MAMA AND PAPA,

. . . On Wednesday morning I signed on and shopped, and spent most of the afternoon consulting with Mr. Coolidge about courses, with the result that my schedule is much altered. I am now taking History, Government, French, English, Latin and Geology, 5½ courses in all. Yesterday I went to Boston in the morning and did some shopping—bought some evening shoes, derby hat, went to the bank, etc. In the P.M. I went to the first lecture, in English, and then saw the foot-ball practice. At 8:30 I went to the Sturgises where there was a grand reunion and welsh rabbit and didn't get back until 11:30. . . .

Papers, I, 429.

He continued to participate in athletics during his first two years. He was no better at football, however, than he had been at Groton—always on practice teams, and always getting bruised and battered by heftier players.

October, 1900

. . . I left the Freshman team on Saturday . . . As I wished to continue playing, I put my name down for one of the 8 scrub teams which are to play until Nov, for a cup. We had our first practice yesterday and I was elected Captain of the Team. It is the only one composed of Freshmen and I am the only Freshman Captain. . . . I am also trying for the Crimson and if I work hard for two years I may be made an Editor. . . .

Later . . . I have had most of the skin on my left hand kicked off in foot-ball, but it is not bad. . . .

Letters, I, 430–431.

At Campobello with Eleanor, 1904

Since he was obviously not built for football he tried rowing; but, although he was now developing a good chest and shoulders, he never had the weight to make the Varsity crew. He had to be content with such games as tennis and golf. At these too he was only fair. But they gave him pleasure, if not honors, and helped him to develop physically.

The Harvard he entered in 1900 had a special personality.

In the courses it offered and in the men who taught them, the Harvard of 1900 was brilliant and liberal. In its social life it was brilliant. Endicott Peabody often decried [and, being an official preacher to the University, spoke out against] the "gap between Mt. Auburn Street and the Yard." In and around Mt. Auburn Street were such expensive dormitories as Westmorly Court [where F.D.R. lived] and such exclusive clubs as the Fly [which F.D.R. made] and the Porcellian [which he did not]; on the other side of Massachusetts Avenue lay the Yard, possessing buildings, badly in need of repair, where lived those who could not afford better—and they were the majority. Financial security and family background very definitely made a difference in all non-scholastic undergraduate activities. Except for friendships which grew up out of common interests at class, and the premier sports of football and crew, there were few opportunities for students of different social spheres to come into normal contact. Graduates of such preparatory schools as Groton usually ate [as Freshmen] at their own special tables in Cambridge eating houses, not in the large common dining halls. Sophomore and Junior societies and the exclusive Senior "final" clubs drew from these ranks. In F.D.R.'s day, the Harvard Union made tentative steps toward bridging the gap, but in essence no foundation for democracy in the social sphere was laid. . . .

Letters, I, 419, Note.

Athletics ranked highest in undergraduate estimation in the early 1900's, but there were other activities for those who were always being urged to "go out for something." And Franklin found the one he was most suited for when he became a reporter for the *Crimson,* Harvard's newspaper. He worked hard at this, and in his senior year, he became the editor.

Ascension unto power on the *Crimson* went something like this: Candidates began to heel the paper as soon as they entered College; starting after the Freshman mid-year, and continuing into Sophomore year, candidates were elected by the Board of Editors; at the beginning of the Junior year two of the successful competitors were elected Assistant Managing Editors; and at the Junior mid-year one of these was named Managing Editor for the rest of the year, becoming the head man on *Crimson* for his class; at the beginning of the Senior year, the Managing Editor became President of the paper, and the remaining Assistant Manager replaced him; then for the second half of the Senior year, a similar shifting of positions took place, with the President retiring into a supervisory position. F.D.R. and Russel Bowie held these last described positions for the class of 1904.

Letters, I, 478, *Note.*

During his last two years at Harvard, Franklin spent nearly half the hours of most days at the *Crimson*, assigning stories to younger candidates, writing editorials, overseeing the make-up of the paper. With all his other activities, and this too, it was remarkable that he was able to study at all. And this becomes more true when it is understood how busy his social life was and how many journeys he made away from college.

CAMBRIDGE
Jan. 6, 1902

. . . On Friday Aunt Kassie, P. C. and M. D. R. and I took the train at 10:50 and had a very comfortable journey to Washington. I went straight to the Keans, and from there, in obedience to Cousin Bammie's note, to the Townsend's tea, which was interesting and filled with New Yorkers whom I knew. I dined at the Keans, [old Mrs.] and there were 40 there. Then to the dance, which was most glorious fun. The Washington people weren't in it with the New Yorkers . . . We left at 2 A.M. and I slept until 12 on Saturday. After lunch Mr. Kean took me over the new Congressional Library and at 4 I went to the White House for tea and stayed till 6. All most interesting. We dined quietly, and at 10 went to the Austrian Ambassador's reception, where I saw many diplomats. On Sunday I went to church with the Keans, and afterwards went again to the White House. . . .

Letters: Early Years.

The people mentioned in this letter were relatives or family friends. They are mentioned again and again in his letters. It was a close and exclusive circle.

By the time he was an upperclassman and had passed twenty, he was handsome and popular. He had not been taken into the very best club, only the second best, and he had not made a varsity team. Still, he had done well enough, and many another student would have been satisfied. But Franklin was, as always, anxious to get to the very top, and his failure to get there was a nagging dissatisfaction. There was one compensation: he was usually successful in getting elected to positions that were voted on. In this way he became the chairman of numerous committees and president of several organizations.

In spite of his outside activities and his average marks he learned much that would be useful to him when he was in public office. His courses were with some of the most noted American scholars, including W. Z. Ripley, the economist, and Archibald Carey Coolidge, the historian, who was also his adviser. Since classes in those days were small, and there was a good deal of argument and group discussion, Franklin's neglect of serious reading was made up for by what he learned from discussion in class.

Actually, he had accumulated enough credits for graduation at the end of three years rather than the usual four. When it had to be decided at the end of his third year what would be done with the fourth, he himself chose to postpone the study of law until he knew more about history, economics and government. His mother disapproved, but he remained firm.

DEAREST MAMA,

I am now fully in the Graduate School—too deep to get out
or change my mind. I am taking five courses in the Department
of History and Political Economy—which interests me much
more than English, but which is also much harder. I have few
hopes of getting an A.M.—indeed I am quite indifferent about
it, but the courses will do me a lot of good. . . .

Letters: Early Years.

It can be seen that he must have been bright enough to
make up for the lack of application to his studies. This had
a later significance. A working politician never has time to
consider any subject thoroughly; he has to pick up what he
can from a little reading and from discussion with those
around him. Even policies of importance have to be decided
without thorough preparation by the decision-maker himself.
The trick of understanding without really mastering subjects
is essential. No one was ever more adept at it than Franklin.

In this fourth year something else happened that his mother
discovered with tight-lipped disapproval. He fell in love with
a girl he had met at a dance, and announced that he intended
to marry her. The girl was Eleanor, the daughter of Theodore's
brother Elliot, and therefore a Roosevelt too. She had had a
difficult girlhood. Her mother had died at an early age and her
father only a little later. She was an affectionate child, and had
been much attached to her father and grieved by a weakness
he had for drink. She had gone, even before her father died,
to live with her grandmother at Tivoli, an estate farther up the
Hudson from Springwood. The elderly lady was meticulous in
her duty to the girl in her charge, but there was little affection
in her program. Eleanor was given over to severe governesses
until she was sent to an exclusive school in England. There she
acquired social graces and a command of French but little
knowledge of academic subjects. She was subdued by the disci-

pline, and her instincts to love and be of service had little opportunity to express themselves.

Eleanor had several personal problems. One was that, as an orphan, she was more or less a nuisance to the family. Another was her undoubted homeliness. She was oversized and awkward, and she had prominent teeth and an unpleasant voice. With these handicaps it was doubtful that she could hope to make the early marriage she was trained for and so retire into matronly obscurity. She was sufficiently intelligent, but she accepted her relatives' opinion that she was unattractive, and she was always fearful that she would be disapproved of more than she seemed to be already. This made her meek as well as awkward.

Franklin had met her on various occasions while they were children; but when he was twenty-two and she was twenty they had not seen each other for years, and they met almost as strangers. His immediate attraction to her was for Eleanor a wonderful and unexpected surprise. She had become resigned to being an extra guest at parties—a Roosevelt, to be sure, but not one the family was proud of. Franklin saw in her a freshness and vigor that outweighed her plain features. She was sympathetic, too, and considerate. If she was not beautiful, she had vitality and an eager mind.

But Franklin's mother considered Eleanor no suitable match for Franklin, and she had no intention of resigning her care of him to a wife, especially to one so undesirable. She took measures. As soon as she was told of Franklin's intention, she lured him away on a six-week trip to Panama.

THE HARVARD CRIMSON
Jan. 30, 1904

DEAREST MAMA,

. . . I have just heard from E. that Mr. and Mrs. Parish have gone away and I couldn't see her (no chaperone) if I went to N.Y. on Wednesday. I find I can get off from here Tuesday night and I feel I must see all I can of E. these last few days— so I am telegraphing you tonight to see if you won't have her

29

up to Hyde Park—coming Wednesday *a.m.* and staying until Thursday. Nobody need know a thing about it and she wouldn't be any trouble as far as getting off is concerned—for I can pack all my things in half an hour. If you decide not to telegraph her I think I must go down on Thursday so as to have all day Friday with her. . . .

Letters, I, 526.

The mother and son made the trip; it disappointed the mother's hopes that it would divert her son's attention from Eleanor; but it resulted in enthusiasm for the vast Panama Canal project that had later results.

Having finished with Harvard Franklin entered the Law School at Columbia University that fall. He was, to this extent, carrying out the program set for him by his father and approved by his mother. His revolt was preparing but was not yet fully developed.

(*5*)

UNCLE Ted, who was so admired by Franklin, had some qualities that the younger man lacked. At Harvard he had won membership in Phi Beta Kappa, and very early developed a gift for writing that was to result in a full shelf of books. The subjects he wrote about ranged from naval history to ecology and, naturally, included public affairs and politics. Franklin was far from being Uncle Ted's equal as a writer, but he was not ready to admit that. He, too, was a Roosevelt, and why might he not have the same gifts?

In 1900 Uncle Ted ran for the Vice-Presidency on the Republican ticket with McKinley; and when McKinley was assassinated in 1901, he became President. In 1904 he was the Republican candidate for a term of his own. The younger Roosevelt followed these developments with enormous interest. Uncle Ted's career had much to do with his own decision to follow a political career; what one Roosevelt had done another could do—and perhaps be even more successful.

Uncle Ted was not accepted by the sons of wealthy families as the safest candidate the Republicans might have nominated in 1904. During his three years in the White House as McKinley's successor, he had disturbed some of the more conservative members of his party. After the quiet dignity of McKinley, he was altogether too talkative. He had especially frightened the big businessmen who were the party's backers by threatening governmental regulation. He spoke of "malefactors of great wealth," a phrase aimed at those who controlled the enormous trusts then in the process of being formed. This sort of talk seemed to make him more a Progressive than a Republican. That leaning was not lost on his younger relative.

Franklin had learned from his professors a good deal about government and the economic system, but he learned also that leadership made the whole system go. And leadership in politics, when it is analyzed, consists mostly of an ability to attract and keep the support of the voters. At this, Uncle Ted was a master. Franklin probably learned more from observing him than he did from his professors. Nevertheless, his fourth year of study was a valuable one. He was right in predicting that he would not get a master's degree, but his studies were more concentrated and practical than they had been in other years.

He spent the summer of 1904 at Hyde Park and Campobello, during this time convincing his reluctant mother that he was determined to marry Eleanor, whatever she thought. Their engagement was finally announced.

His Law School courses at Columbia that fall were taken much as he had taken his undergraduate courses at Harvard. Studying hardly seems to have been his main occupation. He was a gay attendant at innumerable balls and parties; and he and Eleanor were often entertained.

Among the diversions of that year were the doings in Washington as Uncle Ted was inaugurated. This was a kind of preliminary to the young people's wedding in June at the Roosevelt house on East Sixty-fifth Street in New York, when Uncle Ted was present as an expression of his fondness for both of them. The excitement of having a President give the bride away almost obscured the purpose of the occasion; but if Franklin felt any resentment, it was not spoken of.

An otherwise marvelous honeymoon in Europe was slightly marred by the news that Franklin had failed in two of his courses; but this was not allowed to change any plans; and before the university opened in the fall, he had taken make-up examinations and was again in good standing.

The young couple settled down in the first of several houses they would occupy on the upper East Side of New York City. Eleanor found that while she had been away, her mother-in-

Honeymoon at St. Moritz, Switzerland, 1905,
with FDR's aunt, Mrs. Stanley Mortimer

law had attended to the furnishing of a house and had hired a full staff of servants. This was an annoyance since she had the usual desire of a young bride to make her own home and look out for her husband. But this was only the first of many such interferences by the old lady. For many years Eleanor would be subject to Sara's management, a situation made worse by her own incompetence as a housewife. She never did learn to do anything useful in the house and was often in tears because of her frustrations.

When, as they often did, she and Franklin visited Hyde Park, she was little more than a visitor. Even after the children were born her status did not improve. And since there were numerous nurses and governesses, she was less a mother than an onlooker as they grew up. Later in life she wrote of Hyde Park in this fashion:

> I remember Hyde Park on so many, many occasions, covering forty-odd years. I first remember going to the big house when I was a timid young girl not yet engaged to Franklin Delano Roosevelt; he had brought me there to meet his mother's relatives . . . A year later, I remember our honeymoon there—ten days alone in the house, still closed for the winter, except for the Scotch laundress-maid, Elsie, who cooked our meals for us . . . I remember going back every spring and autumn, with our growing family of energetic children . . . I particularly recall being there for part of the year when Franklin, at thirty-nine, was stricken with polio. . . . Later, I remember going to Hyde Park when he was Governor of New York State, and then for all the years in the 1930s and early 1940s, when the old mansion was known as the Summer White House. How filled were the guest rooms with the famous statesmen of this country and of the world! . . . And I remember returning on April 15, 1945, on the funeral train from Washington, D.C., when my husband was laid to rest in the rose garden, close to the house in which he had been born and which he had loved so well for all his sixty-three years.
>
> Some of the events I remember in connection with the house are emotional ones, all but invisible at the time—such as my own gradual change from an awkwardly uncertain young woman,

completely under the domination of others, into an independent personality. For it was against the background of Hyde Park that I slowly did what every human being must eventually do: I learned the lessons of adaptability and adjustment, then of self-reliance—and finally, although it took me a very long time to grow up, I became an individual in my own right.

But here I must confess that, despite all my memories of life at Hyde Park, in one sense I think this memoir could well be titled "I Remember My Mother-in-Law's Hyde Park." It was indeed her home, and she made every decision concerning it. For over forty years, I was only a visitor there, which is the reason I never had a feeling of personal ownership toward the house. Naturally, Franklin felt more of a sense of possession than I did, although he actually owned Hyde Park for only the four years between his mother's death and his own. But, of course, he always knew that, by the terms of his father's will, his mother could not sell the Hyde Park property without his consent and that someday it would belong to him.

McCall's, February, 1963, 72 (published after her death).

At Campobello, during the summer, it was the same. Sara bought the younger people a house next door to hers, and her control of family affairs was seldom relaxed.

For Franklin this arrangement was something of a convenience. While his mother was busy managing households, she was too busy to manage him. It seems selfish of him to have left Eleanor in this situation; but nothing was ever done about it. Actually, it was some time before he had any decisions of importance to make. He had first to complete his law work and go through the usual apprenticeship. If he had any further ambitions, they had to wait. But it is obvious that all along he had something in mind that his mother would not like any better than she had liked his marriage. When he was finished with Law School (he did not graduate or even bother to complete the courses of his last year, having that spring passed the examinations for the Bar), he became a clerk in the respectable Wall Street firm of Carter, Ledyard and Milburn.

An incident in that office was afterward recalled by Gren-

Franklin and Eleanor with Anna and James, 1908

ville Clark, an associate. One day, as Franklin and the other clerks were discussing their ambitions, he remarked that he wasn't going to practice law forever. He intended to get into politics and run for office at the first opportunity. He even thought he had a very good chance to become President. To Mr. Clark, who told about this years later, when Franklin had indeed become President, it seemed a remarkable prophecy for a young man to make about himself.

If, while he was a young lawyer, his mother still hoped he would become a country gentleman, knowing enough law to look after the estate, but otherwise not attempting to develop a career, she was disappointed. In 1910, the Democratic politicians of his district, which included Dutchess County, proposed to Franklin that he become a candidate for the state legislature; and he left the practice of law for politics, with every sign of eager ambition. It was in much the same way that Uncle Ted had got his start. True, no Democrat had ever been elected from that district. But he could try. It was one way to begin:

> He broke precedent spectacularly by hiring a red Maxwell touring car, decking it out with flags, and setting out . . . to tour every corner of the district. Calamity howlers predicted that he would scare farmers' horses and thus lose more votes than he could possibly gain. But the car was a strategic asset as well as a gaudy advertisement in which they could roll along at about twenty-two miles an hour. Without it they could not possibly have covered the area in four weeks. Roosevelt remembered, "When we met a horse or a team—and that was every half mile or so—we had to stop, not only the car but the engine as well." They made an asset of this by exchanging political banter with each teamster as he passed. They also talked to farmers husking corn, sitting around country stores, or lounging at crossroads . . .
>
> Friedel, *Roosevelt,* 91.

Even if he were defeated, he would learn something; but he had no intention of losing for lack of hard work. He covered his district energetically, making many speeches a day and reaching nearly all the voters. There seems to be some doubt whether his brash campaign was a help or a hindrance. But he won.

(**6**)

EVERYONE was surprised when Franklin was elected. The circumstances seemed to arrange themselves so that he could hardly lose. And the ally of most importance was Uncle Ted, who was not on the scene at all. Even at a distance his influence was felt in upstate New York as well as in the rest of the country. He had retired from the Presidency in 1909, but he now had a strong feeling that he had left public life too early. He was not at all happy as an observer and commentator; and his literary work did not satisfy his restless longing to be at the center of affairs. Besides, President Taft, his successor, had turned out to be far more conservative than he could approve. He hoped to convert the Republicans to Progressivism; but he knew how strong the Old Guard was in the party and what a fight he would have to make if he were to succeed. Nevertheless, it was a decision he meant to carry out in the campaign of 1912.

In 1910 Theodore had already begun to assert himself as the leader of an attempt to capture the Republican Party and the Progressive movement. This immediately split the Republican party even though the Presidential election was still two years away.

Democrats, even local ones in upstate New York, were helped by their rivals' quarrels. So, although Franklin was young and unpracticed, he was elected.

What happened next illustrates a shrewdness that he always showed in politics. He had no sooner taken his Senate seat than he joined with a group of Democratic rebels in opposing election of Tammany's candidate to the United States Senate. At that time, United States Senators were still elected by state legislatures. Charles F. Murphy, the Tammany boss, who considered that he controlled the legislature, had promised the Senatorship to "Blue-eyed Billy" Sheehan. This he thought was only a fair return for Sheehan's efforts in gathering campaign funds from various public utilities and thus helping the Democrats to win. But those utilities would expect other privileges when Sheehan became Senator; and the rebel group opposed themselves to the alliance between the party and these favor-seekers. Sheehan found himself in the center of the fight that followed.

Franklin knew that there would be public reaction if this sort of deal became public. He also knew that a young politician might become favorably known for protesting so blatant a purchase of public office. There might be the possibility, in this, of convincing a wide audience that he was a hero. Of course there was also the danger that the powerful Tammany organization would punish him when it got the chance. This might even result in his not being renominated in 1912, since the Dutchess County organization from which he came was closely affiliated with the New York City organization. But he took the chance, and for several weeks he and his associates were able to hold up all legislative business until their demands were met. They finally gained a compromise of sorts. Supreme Court Judge O'Gorman was chosen Senator instead of Sheehan. O'Gorman was a Tammany man too; so Tammany had not been wholly defeated; the newspapers, however, counted it a success for the rebels, and Boss Murphy was embarrassed.

It happened that Franklin alone among the hold-outs had a house in Albany. With Eleanor as hostess, it became a convenient meeting place; and naturally Franklin became the spokesman when statements were issued and bargains discussed. He was thus given credit for being the leader. He hardly deserved this; but he took full advantage of it. From being, in January, an obscure young first-term legislator, he was by April known throughout the state, and even elsewhere, as a rising crusader for good government, willing to oppose the sinister deals of the bosses.

FDR and Elliott at Campobello, 1912

The reporter who did most to publicize Franklin's part in this incident was Louis McHenry Howe, Albany correspondent of the New York *Tribune*. This was the beginning of a long association. Howe was to continue serving Franklin in this same way from then on, pushing, managing his publicity, and subordinating his own interests to the furthering of Franklin's.

Although some of the other conspirators against Tammany were punished by being passed over in 1912, Franklin's reputation was so great that his renomination could not be prevented. He was also re-elected, since the Republicans were having even more serious quarrels among themselves than they had had in 1910. In 1912 Uncle Ted took more than half the Republican voters out of the party and into his Bull Moose movement (the Progressive Party), when the Republican nomination was refused him. As a result, Woodrow Wilson, the Democratic candidate, was elected to the Presidency.

Meanwhile, Franklin's political foresight had again been demonstrated. Just after his tangle with Tammany, having by then become widely known, he went to call on Wilson, who was at that time Governor of New Jersey. Franklin had made the shrewd guess that Wilson would be the next Democratic candidate and that, because of Republican troubles, he would be elected. Most observers at the time would have said that Senator Harmon of Ohio or Speaker Champ Clark of Missouri would be more likely candidates. Or they might well have thought that the Republicans would win the election, as they had won most elections since the Civil War (Cleveland's two victories in 1884 and 1892 being the exceptions). But Franklin judged differently. He offered Wilson his support.

This cannot have been regarded by Wilson as a very valuable offer. Whatever Franklin promised, Tammany would still control the New York delegation to the coming Presidential convention in Baltimore. But it did put Franklin on record. And when Wilson had been nominated after a hard fight and elected, he recalled the young upstate legislator's enthusiasm. Josephus Daniels, an ardent Wilson supporter who was joining the Cabinet as Secretary of the Navy, had noticed Franklin's enthusiasm, too. He proposed the young man for the Assistant Secretaryship in his Department. Wilson agreed, and the nomination was made.

Franklin's departure from Albany and entrance into a Federal post in Washington enabled him not only to escape the continuing opposition of Tammany in New York but also to pursue an old enthusiasm for the Navy. There had been a time when he had tried to persuade his parents that he ought to go to the Naval Academy. They had said no. Now, when he was thirty-one, he was to become a member of the Navy Department, if not a naval officer, and his old ambition would find a certain satisfaction.

He resigned his New York State senatorship. He and Eleanor moved to Washington, where they were to live for eight years in the same R Street house that Uncle Ted had occupied while he was Assistant Secretary of the Navy.

Franklin naturally hoped that this identity in beginning would lead to the same result. Uncle Ted had used the position of Assistant Secretary in his climb to the Presidency. Why not another Roosevelt?

(7)

FRANKLIN had never been an administrator before he started in at the Navy Department, and he had to learn as he went along. He did not enjoy working at a desk, but his confinement was relieved by association with the Navy officers he admired and by visits to the yards where ships were built. He went on many practice cruises and watched maneuvers with the commanders. To him this was as exciting as any experience of his life.

Since summers in Washington were hot, it was fashionable for officials to have vacation homes elsewhere. Franklin sent the family away, usually to Campobello, and visited them when he could. In the fall they all gathered again in the R Street house. There were rumors then, and in later years, that during the summer of 1913 he was much attracted to a Lucy Mercer, a friend of Eleanor. But the rumors were never substantiated.

The Roosevelts moved in a lively society of younger officials and foreign diplomats, among whom were several who were to become prominent in politics—Herbert Hoover, for instance, who was then Food Administrator. And there were several young foreign attachés who later became ambassadors when Franklin was President. There were receptions, dinners, or parties nearly every night; but the Roosevelts were used to this sort of life and would hardly have known what to do without it.

Franklin's work began in 1913, and the war in Europe began in 1914. The peacetime Navy had always cherished the ambition to expand. Although the United States was not to be at war for several years, the Navy officers were immensely excited by the probability of involvement in the war so obvi-

42

ously imminent in Europe. They were unanimous in believing that the nation would in time have to join with Britain, and they were increasingly eager for more men and more ships. Franklin caught their fever. He talked more than he should have about an expanded Navy while President Wilson was holding to a policy of neutrality—and so, he got into trouble. He seemed to forget that as a subordinate he had a duty to support his Chief.

Much of his seven years as Assistant Secretary seems to have been spent either in trying to escape his civilian job and become a naval officer, or in trying to be nominated for some elective office back in New York State. He did not succeed in either ambition, but it was not from lack of trying.

Before the United States got into the war, he tried to capture the nomination for a senatorship from New York. He did it, however, without the approval of Navy Secretary Daniels or of President Wilson, and so he got no help from them, and was badly defeated in the primary. This was the start of differences with his superiors that became worse as more and more openly he became an advocate of naval expansion and, presently, of declaring war.

He had found immediately after his appointment that an Assistant Secretary is no very exalted official in Washington; and perhaps this had something to do with his desire for a change. No alternative appeared, so he tried to get noticed in other ways. This is something a younger official with political ambitions will often do. But it seldom succeeds. If he becomes conspicuous, his superiors will regard him with suspicion; and if he does not, he is just another among many minor people in a big bureaucracy. Real political ambitions are best satisfied by elective office; and to achieve that, a man is almost required to resign whatever appointive position he may hold in order to become a candidate. If he succeeds, he will win an independence he can never have as an appointed official and will command corresponding respect.

Franklin was of two minds. He wanted an elective office; but he felt it his duty to help in the campaign for a bigger

With Theodore Douglas Robinson in Washington, 1913

On an inspection tour, 1915

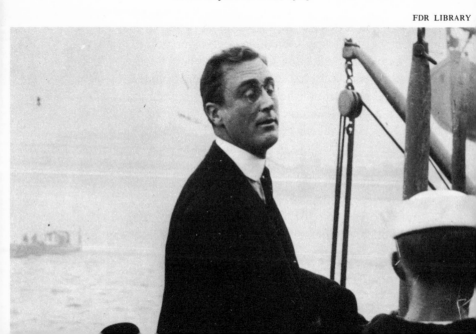

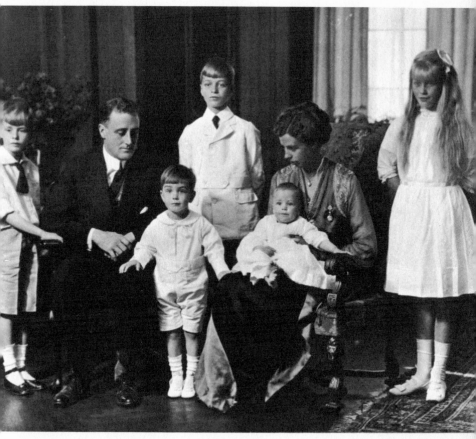

FDR and his family in Washington, 1916

Navy and for entrance into the war. Then, somewhat later, when the war had started, he felt that he ought to be in active service. Anyone who had not worn uniform would be under a handicap in the postwar political world. (This was why Uncle Ted had resigned from the Navy Department at the beginning of the Spanish-American War and organized the Rough Riders.)

But time passed. Franklin's attempts to get into politics failed. When he might have become a junior officer, Daniels appealed to him to go on with his Departmental work. There was an immense Naval expansion; much of the war threatened to be at sea, and the Navy had to carry out its assignment. So he stayed.

Before President Wilson began to give up his policy of neutrality and while Franklin was rather openly advocating war, Wilson began to consider disciplining him. Wilson's displeasure was made worse by Franklin's rather openly expressed opinions about Secretary Daniels. That older politician from North Carolina was a gentleman of a sort Franklin was not used to. He was a Southerner from what is sometimes spoken of as the "Bible Belt," and he took his church teachings seriously. For instance, he was a temperance advocate, and he ordered the Navy to stop serving alcohol. In the officers' messes not even wine could be served. Daniels was a plain and modest man who wore string ties, a broad hat, and square-toed shoes. This made a picture Harvard graduates found easy to ridicule, and Franklin was among those who spoke slightingly of him, as in this letter to Eleanor in 1913.

To my astonishment on reaching the Dept. nobody seemed the least bit excited about the European crisis—Mr. Daniels feeling chiefly sad that his faith in human nature and civilization and similar idealistic nonsense was receiving such a rude shock. So I started in alone to get things ready and prepare plans for what *ought* to be done by the navy . . .

These dear good people like W.J.B. [William Jennings Bryan] and J.D. [Josephus Daniels] have as much conception of what a general European war means as Elliott has of higher mathematics [Elliott was his small son].

Personal Letters.

Daniels actually was a shrewd and effective politician, trusted by members of the Congress much more than a Secretary of more sophisticated appearance would have been. But during the period of neutrality, Daniels' strict acceptance of the President's policy, together with his plain manners and his enforcement of temperance, led to a good deal of ridicule from the press and from people prominent in capital society. This makes it the more remarkable that he was always kind, tolerant, and encouraging to Franklin. Moreover, he defended the younger man when Wilson might have dismissed him. But of course, everything was changed when war was declared and there was a call for naval action.

Franklin soon discovered how often Daniels got the appropriations he asked for from the Congress. He was forced to revise his estimate of the man, and before long he was suitably ashamed of his past opinions. From then on he and the Secretary worked very well together.

Franklin was aided in becoming an efficient Secretary by the presence of Louis Howe in the next office. Howe had followed him from Albany—would always follow him from then on. Much of the good opinion Franklin accumulated among Democratic politicians was owed to Howe's unremitting service. He cultivated politicians, newspapermen, and other influential people and kept them aware of Franklin's existence. This gradually expanded to a country-wide recognition.

Before the war was over, Franklin had learned to carry really enormous responsibilities. Considering that he had been wholly new at such work in 1913, his performance was impressive. He learned rapidly; and if President Wilson never really got over his prejudice against him, he was at least accepted as a useful member of the war organization. Daniels was more and more his mentor and friend.

When the war was in its last stage, Franklin was at last

47

allowed to go abroad to see conditions for himself. He had been eager to get closer to the fighting, but his requests had been ignored. When he finally was allowed to go, he got as close to the front lines as he could. This experience excited him so that he made a final effort to imitate Uncle Ted. He conceived the idea of commanding a battery of heavy naval guns mounted on railway cars. He went to the President's office as soon as he could get back to Washington and asked permission to take a commission. Wilson told him he was too late. An armistice had been proposed and would be signed before his project could be organized.

Then, when the war ended, Wilson went abroad to negotiate the peace treaty with the defeated enemy. Franklin followed Wilson to Paris on naval business and saw something of the proceedings. He returned on the same ship that brought Wilson back in the spring, and, although the President was terribly tired from his efforts and had to rest during much of the voyage, he did talk with Franklin several times.

The President spoke of his desire to establish a world organization that would keep the peace in the future. He had bargained hard with the heads of the other governments who were more interested in the extension of their empires than in any such enterprise. By conceding much of what they demanded, although he believed it unwise, Wilson had won their agreement to the League of Nations. He regarded this as the only hope for a peaceable world.

Wilson's goal and his exhaustion in the effort to see it come to pass moved Franklin deeply; it was for him almost a conversion, and something that would have immense consequences at a future time. From a belligerent young man, working hard to destroy an enemy, he became quite suddenly an ardent advocate of international order. The leader he had not served too faithfully in the past had won him over.

When Wilson failed in his attempt to gain United States acceptance for the treaty embodying the League, Franklin was distressed. There were still isolationists in the Senate and Republicans who opposed the President for political reasons.

Arriving at the U.S. Naval Air Station, Pauillac, France, 1918

On a cross-country speaking tour for this purpose, Wilson broke down, and for the rest of his life he was an invalid. The treaty never did command the necessary two-thirds vote in the Senate for ratification.

Franklin shared Wilson's disappointment. He made the League a major issue of his campaign for Vice-President in 1920, but, more important, the idea would remain dormant within him, and he never gave up his conviction that the time would come when some international organization could be established. And when Franklin became President his conversion by Wilson at last had its result. American participation in World War II was predicated on the agreement, from the first, to a peace organization named, of course, the United Nations.

49

(8)

IN the summer of 1920, when the Democrats met in San Francisco to nominate their new Presidential candidate, the Party was in sorry shape. Its leader, Wilson, was sick and discredited; the country had had enough of his idealism and seemed to feel no gratitude for his leadership during the war. A few weeks earlier, the Republicans had nominated Warren Harding for President and Calvin Coolidge for Vice-President, and though this was a weak slate (and the Democrats knew it), their platform based on a "return to normalcy" was a popular one. So when the Democratic delegates convened, they did so with little hope of victory.

In a desultory convention, marked mostly by a vague desire to nominate a man far removed from Wilson's influence, the delegates chose James M. Cox, Ohio Governor, as their Presidential candidate and, just as they were about to leave, Franklin D. Roosevelt for Vice-President.

Franklin won the nomination for several reasons. First, he was allied, however loosely, with the Wilson administration, and the delegates felt they could not sever ties with Wilson altogether. Second, he was not considered radically progressive on domestic matters. And finally, he was no longer opposed by Tammany boss Charles E. Murphy, who seemed to feel that it was better to have Franklin a losing Vice-Presidential candidate than a winning candidate for a New York governorship.

Franklin accepted the nomination gladly. He seems to have felt that he and Cox stood a chance to win; but even if he lost, he would at least have gained national prominence and a right to Democratic support when conditions for the Party improved.

Cox and Roosevelt made the League of Nations their major campaign issue. It was consistent with their beliefs, but politically fatal, even though it is doubtful whether they would have won even if they had stayed clear of the issue.

In November, 1920, Franklin waited for returns in his big house at Springwood, just as he would after more successful campaigns when he himself was the Presidential candidate. Springwood was a mansion now, extensively enlarged and quite changed in appearance. It had the look of an important man's home.

On this occasion—as he would on later ones—he seated himself at one end of the long mahogany table in the dining room and began to make tabulations as soon as the first election news started to come in from the eastern states.

In 1920 there was a special telegraph line; by 1932 there would be clacking teletype machines; and there would always be the almost unendurable excitement of election night.

He always waited with pretended indifference; but only pretended. This was the pay-off, the most important thing that happened in a politician's career. He and his assistants always made bets on the result. The closest guesser won a pool. Franklin was apt to underestimate his own drawing power; and his guess was not usually the closest. It is recorded by Tom Lynch, then New York State Tax Commissioner and worker in that first campaign, that when it was obvious—almost immediately—that the election was lost, Franklin remarked, "Well anyway, I figured that 1932 would be my year."

This did not seem a very intelligent forecast to Lynch or the others in the room. The defeat of Cox and Roosevelt was so overwhelming that to hope for a Democratic victory in any of the next few elections seemed hopelessly unrealistic. If Franklin thought there might be a chance of victory as soon as 1932, he was probably the only one who did. Afterward,

At the ballpark with friends, 1917

FDR in his boat at Campobello, circa 1918

FDR at Hyde Park, accepting Vice-Presidential nomination, 1920

Campaigning with James Cox, 1920

Lynch recalled the prophecy with some awe—as well he might. It was uncannily accurate.

After the returns came in, the neighbors from the surrounding countryside paraded to the house by torchlight and gathered on the broad Springwood lawn. It was a defeat, but they came anyway. Franklin went out to say a few words and to shake a good many hands. These friends were the first to see him, as in other election years. They could not know that it would be the only election lost in seven—this one, two for the governorship, and four for the Presidency.

The newspapers were then, as always during Franklin's time, mostly Republican, and they were jubilant. Harding's victory would result in a return to a safe and conservative policy. There would be no "foreign entanglements." People could go about their affairs quite certain that nothing disturbing would happen in Washington.

It is quite clear that by election time Franklin did not really expect a victory; and he must have been considering that defeat would begin for him a period when he would be out of public life. He could not expect any appointment, naturally; and no Democrat would be elected to a national office at any time soon. He also knew, however, that there was a rhythm in American politics. In spite of the Republican dominance since the Civil War, Cleveland and Wilson had been able to win, and each had won a second term. Both, it is true, had been minority Presidents, winning with less than half of the popular vote. But their successes were significant.

Something of the sort would happen again. It was likely, he felt, that the Republicans would become corrupt or careless or split on some issue as they had before. Cleveland and Wilson had been able to take advantage of such situations. Franklin could at least prepare himself to do the same.

First, however, he must find a job. He had a personal problem at the moment. He was short of money. The Roosevelts had always lived luxuriously, but their fortune was relatively small. They were used to large houses with many servants, governesses for small children, and private schools for older ones, with several cars and boats; and with a summer house. Their private income often would not meet all the bills. Franklin's mother was still mistress at Springwood and paid its large costs, but he had the house in New York—and all those expensive children!

He could practice law. That might be the best thing!—and he did arrange to join a law firm, but then was offered a position as vice-president of the Fidelity and Deposit Company of Maryland—in their New York office. This was a large concern whose business was insuring firms against risks of loss from theft or defalcation, and Franklin would be useful mostly because his political connections would help to bring in business. The salary was $25,000 a year; and this was more certain than a lawyer's fees. It would keep his expensive family going. He was glad to accept.

So while a Republican was sitting at his old Navy Department desk, Franklin was getting started in Wall Street as a lawyer and businessman. But his job was one that would enable him to keep up a large correspondence, go to political meetings, and keep himself available. That was his plan for the years just ahead—to let people know that he would be ready to run whenever the time was favorable for a Democrat.

As he thought over the campaign just past, he considered that, although it had been lost, he had done all the right things. Certainly he need not be ashamed. The political atmosphere had excited and stimulated him. Speaking trips had been planned and organized so that there was always a crowd. There had been a special train and, hitched to it, a special car for the candidate, to be lived in for weeks at a time. He had spoken from the back platform in small towns; and, in big ones, at cheering Democratic rallies. Just as important, he had had long and intimate talks with many local political leaders. They had told him their problems, and he had listened to each as though he never expected to hear anything more important.

Of him it might really be said that a campaign was a vacation, although it might seem a terrible ordeal to others. Now that it was over he was tired, but he had enjoyed it. He had been doing what he was meant to do.

In this campaign he had behaved, as several commentators observed, as though he and not Cox were the Presidential candidate. He had crossed the nation several times; he had spoken on many subjects; and, actually, he had emerged as the leading Democrat in the country. He had only to hold the prominence he had gained.

His hard work in the midst of discouraging circumstances had served the Party well. Cox had been a much less colorful and a less popular campaigner. During the next twelve years, while the Republicans were in the White House, Franklin planned to keep in touch with all the many leaders he had met. He would never let them forget his availability.

The terrible thing that happened a year after he went to work on Wall Street was the first of life's calamities for him. He was stricken with poliomyelitis at Campobello. At first it paralyzed him from the upper chest down; then, only slowly, it relaxed.

No one can say how the mysterious disease was contracted. He had attended a Boy Scout outing at Palisades Interstate Park a week before, and after coming back to Campobello he had slipped on the deck of a boat and had fallen into the cold Bay of Fundy while fishing. He was still tired from several exhausting weeks when his administration of the Navy was being investigated by the Republicans now in office. His tiredness and the chill may have given the disease a chance to develop.

It came on suddenly. One afternoon while the family was sailing in their small yacht, the *Vireo,* they saw a brush fire on an nearby island, and landed to put it out. They worked for some hours, got thoroughly overheated, and then went for a swim. That evening Franklin felt ill and went to bed early. The next morning, he could not stand up and later in the day gradually lost the use of his legs and then of nearly his whole body.

56

The local doctor made a wrong diagnosis; and it was two weeks before a specialist was called in. Until then, he had been given incorrect treatment, and the paralysis had hardly retreated at all. It was not until two weeks after this that he could be taken to New York and hospitalized.

Not much was known about polio then. Even though only his legs continued to be paralyzed, he was naturally depressed by his continued helplessness. His struggle to walk again during the next few years was a continual ordeal. He learned from his own experience more about rehabilitation than anyone had known before.

From a tall, handsome, athletic man, he had become a wheel-chair case, dependent on others even for the simplest movements. His mother saw this as an opportunity. Surely, she thought, the fight for recovery was strain enough. He must not think of going on with a political career, so physically demanding, so wearing even for the most vigorous person. She pleaded with him to relax, to come back to Hyde Park and the life he loved. She would see that he was cushioned with care and that his invalid condition was eased.

Eleanor and Louis Howe differed with her. They felt that even though his legs were helpless he had lost none of his talent. The destiny they had seen for him was still possible to attain if he would only make the commitment.

During the ordeal of striving to recover, he had stubbornly refused to give up. He studied his own symptoms, tried every sort of medicine and exercise—some of these exercises requiring incredible exertions—and gradually realized that he would never regain the use of his legs. He had to go on without them.

The most encouraging of all the cures he had tried—although in the end it did not succeed as he hoped—was exercise in the pools at Warm Springs, Georgia, where warm mineralized waters gushed up from deep in the earth. He made repeated visits there and gradually worked out a regimen that gave him vigorous health even if it did not restore the muscles

57

of his legs. He knew finally that nothing could revive the dead tissues. But he learned that even the most helpless cripple could be aided in regaining a certain independence.

He also found that the mild climate and the restful country-side gave him the most tranquil retreat he had ever found. During the years from 1924, when he first went there, until he died in the Little White House on Pine Mountain at Warm Springs, it was a second home. Almost as much as Spring-wood, it is remembered for its association with him.

When he first went there, he found a rundown resort hotel. He bought it and transformed the whole place into a large center for the rehabilitation of polio victims. When he became President, he gave over its ownership to a foundation so that the work might be carried on. Fortunately, in the future there were to be fewer victims of polio and the center would be more useful to other cripples than to those for whom it was first intended. This was because Franklin was never satisfied merely to rehabilitate; he wanted to prevent polio. So the foundation devoted itself as much to discovering the cause of the disease as to repairing its terrible results. In the end, before Franklin died, it was close to being conquered. If he were responsible for nothing else—this alone would be a magnificent credit for any man.

(9)

A QUARREL between two factions of the Democratic Party—on the one side the old conservative, rural, and Protestant South, and on the other the newer, more progressive, and more predominantly Catholic North and East—was certain to occur sooner or later, as immigrants from southern and eastern Europe enlarged the number of city voters. In the Democratic convention of 1924, all the latent bitterness between the two groups showed itself in a struggle for the nomination.

The convention was held in Madison Square Garden in New York City. It was one of the first to be heard over nation-wide radio networks. Since radio was so new an influence in politics, the delegates may not have understood how important the effect was of their fierce quarreling being heard by millions of voters.

The delegates from the rural South and West had dark suspicions about the intentions of the eastern city people. These were not new, only suddenly made sharper by the religious issue. For the first time a Catholic—Al Smith—was being put forward, and Protestants feared this was evidence of something they had long been warned against. They muttered about "the Pope's influence," and set themselves to resist.

Alfred E. Smith had been Governor of New York and was known for his liberal views and his efficient administration, but he was unmistakably an East Side New Yorker. His accent betrayed his origin, and his brown derby and flashy clothes proclaimed his pride in that origin. It was well known that he owed his career to Tammany Hall and that he was a Catholic.

His strongest opponent was William G. McAdoo of California, who had been Wilson's Secretary of the Treasury. He was backed by the southern and many western delegates; and it was whispered that he was supported by the Ku Klux Klan. McAdoo was as much disliked by the Smith people as Smith was by the McAdoo faction.

Maneuvering for control had begun long before the convention. It was in full knowledge of the dangerous religious issue that Smith asked Franklin Roosevelt to be his preconvention manager. Franklin accepted at once, saying that Democrats who opposed Smith because of his religion could only be called bigots. Catholics were as much citizens as the members of any other church. What was far more important was that Smith had been a successful governor and was in every way a most suitable candidate. This was, in fact, the theme of Roosevelt's later address nominating Smith at the convention. He spoke of his man as "a Happy Warrior" in liberal causes; and even those who opposed Smith recognized the ability of the speaker.

The applause was generous and much of it was for himself. Everyone knew of his three-year battle to recover from the effects of polio. Those who saw him struggle from his chair and advance to the rostrum on the arm of his son James felt that they were witnessing something of a miracle. It was obvious that his legs were useless; he walked on heavy braces, swinging from his hips. But he took hold of the desk before him firmly. His big shoulders and healthy face were as handsome as ever. His tenor voice was as clear and ringing as it had been in 1920 when many of these same delegates had heard him accept the nomination for the Vice-Presidency. He might not be able to stand without help, but there was nothing wrong with his mind!

It was even suggested that so admirable a figure would himself make a good candidate. Nothing came of the suggestion. Franklin would not have wanted it to—but only because it was not yet time. He was still as ambitious as ever. And even the press could sense his power. The New York *Herald Tribune* said:

While the results of the futile ballots were droned from the platform yesterday, there sat in the exact center of the great hall the one man whose name would stampede the convention were he put in nomination. He is the only man to whom the contending factions could turn. . . . And that man does not want the nomination and would be alarmed if he knew what people were saying about him in the delegations. . . . From the time Roosevelt made his speech in nomination of Smith . . . he has been the foremost figure on floor or platform . . . without the slightest desire to do so, he has done for himself what he could not do for his candidate.

After the nominating speeches had been made and the voting had begun, neither of the factions showed any sign of compromise. Heat and exhaustion rasped tempers. Presently the delegates were shouting angrily at each other. Both sides were stubborn and the voting went on and on throughout a sweltering week until seventy ballots had been taken. Only then, when the whole country had been made aware that the Party was deeply divided, did the leaders finally agree on a Wall Street lawyer as a compromise candidate.

This was John W. Davis, who was really wanted by no one and who was destined to defeat. The year 1924 was no more a Democratic one than 1920 had been. The Republicans, on the other hand, had a candidate exactly suited to their desires —Calvin Coolidge. Coolidge was already President, having filled out the term of Harding, who had died two years before. Business was booming. Prosperity, the Republicans said, would continue if Coolidge were kept in the White House. All the voters need do was to "keep cool with Coolidge." And that is what they did.

After the excitement Franklin went back to his job and watched Davis lose the election. He continued his efforts to regain some use of his legs. Twice a year he went to Warm Springs for therapy, still hoping but without much encouragement.

In 1928 he was again a delegate to the Presidential convention, this time in Houston, Texas. Again he made the

left to right: Lt. Governor George Lunn, FDR, Presidential candidate John W. Davis, and Al Smith at Hyde Park, 1924

At Warm Springs, Georgia, circa 1928

nominating speech for Smith. *The New York Times* described the speech this way:

> There was nothing strained or fantastic or extravagant in what Roosevelt said. It was the address of a fair-minded and cultured man, avoiding the usual perils of national convention oratory and discussing in an intelligent way the qualifications which should be sought for in the President of the United States.

Bigotry now was sufficiently weakened to allow a big city Catholic to get the nomination. And Smith went out to campaign.

But the Republicans again had an appealing candidate, Herbert Hoover, who had made such a splendid impression as Food Administrator during the war and who had been Secretary of Commerce since. It was apparent almost at once that Smith had very little chance of winning against "the great engineer." Even Smith himself, being a knowledgeable politician, very soon saw how things were going. He was especially humiliated to discover that he would probably lose even New York State where he had several times been elected to the governorship. Could this be avoided? Possibly, by finding a candidate for the governorship who would hold the upstate areas for the Party.

The man who was most likely to do this was Roosevelt. When the Democratic state convention met in September, its leaders tried to get in touch with him, at Smith's urging, to offer him the nomination. But he was nowhere to be found. Even Eleanor, who was a delegate—showing how interested in politics she had become—was unable to locate him. He was supposed to be in Warm Springs but he had anticipated what was happening and had gone away on a "political trip." He hoped, if there was a delay, some other ambitious person might be chosen. Instead the convention stood adjourned until he could be found.

Meanwhile Louis Howe in New York was frantically sending messages urging Franklin to refuse. This was exactly what

Franklin's own judgment counseled and what he intended to do. He said as much both to Eleanor and Smith when they reached him finally by telephone. He even made a personal appeal: he said it would end his effort to regain control over his legs. He had been making progress at the Springs, and it was unfair, he said, to make him stop. The real reason, of course, was that he realized the hopelessness of the Democratic cause and felt that, if he were involved in the defeat, his career would be ended.

He had been reasoning this way since it had become obvious that Smith would lose. He himself was already a national figure, having been a candidate for the Vice-Presidency and having cultivated so carefully a national following. He would, therefore, be in a better position to be a candidate in a later and more favorable year if he did not risk the loss of a governorship race in 1928.

But Smith and his supporters were tough about it. They told Franklin that if he refused to run he need not expect any future favors from the Party. Since it was put this way, he had to give in. He had no choice.

After his nomination, he came back to New York and made the same sort of lively canvass he had made for the Vice-Presidency in 1920. He was helped by one of Smith's young assistants, Samuel I. Rosenman, who traveled with him and acted as counselor. With Sam's help, Franklin made a speech nearly every day, and sometimes several. Sam told of it later:

> After a speech had been delivered in one city, I sat up and prepared a draft of the speech for the next night. It had to be ready for the candidate to look at the next morning during his breakfast. . . .
>
> After breakfast the cavalcade of cars would start the journey to the next city. I would get into the bus where the typewriters were, and, with Roosevelt's corrections and suggestions, would work on the draft. As each page was finished I would give it to the typists, and they would knock out a clean copy while the bus was in motion. . . .
>
> Generally at noon we stopped an hour or so in a village where

local party leaders had arranged a luncheon. After his im-
promptu speech following the lunch, we usually had an opportunity to go into a private room and turn out the final draft.

Rosenman, 21.

They traveled up and down the state this way for weeks.

It was not easy for a crippled man to carry on this kind of
campaign. It was a strenuous ordeal for him to get in and out of
automobiles and hotels. He made his daytime speeches standing
in the back of his car. The simple job of getting up and sitting
down several times was almost as much exercise as the ordinary
man takes during an entire day. He could not climb stairs and
often we had to carry him up some back stairs of a hall and
down again. He always went through this harrowing experience
smiling. Having been set down he would adjust his coat and
proceed calmly to the platform for his speech. . . . In later years
I was to see the same kind of courage and stamina time and
again; but my wonder never wore off—nor my admiration.

Rosenman, 22.

Franklin did so well that, in spite of the Democratic defeat
in the national election—Smith did not carry New York after
all—Franklin was elected Governor. The margin was small;
but it was decisive.

Now he had another claim on the Party, and he could look
for future payment. If he could win re-election to a second
term as Governor in 1930, he would certainly be chosen as
the candidate for the Presidency in 1932. And he had found
in Sam Rosenman another helper, quite as valuable as Louis
Howe and quite as devoted too.

When the Roosevelt family moved into the Governor's mansion in Albany no one could have known what kind of year
1929 would turn out to be. Within a few months the long
run of prosperity would end in a crash; and the nation would
enter its longest and most disheartening depression. The first
crash would cause billions of dollars in values to disappear as

With his wife and mother at the time of his inauguration as
Governor of New York, 1929

if by evil magic. Speculators who had thought themselves rich one day would find themselves penniless the next. And there were many people with meager funds who had been gambling with their savings. The whole country seemed to be involved. It was hoped that the market would recover, but it was soon evident that more was wrong than anyone had thought at first. And since the Republicans had been claiming credit for the boom, they had to accept the blame for its ending.

During the first months of 1929, what was to occur so soon was no more anticipated by Franklin than by others—except a few economists to whom no one listened. And he began his work in Albany more as a successor to the much-admired Smith than as one who was himself expected to lead. One of his real problems, in fact, was to establish himself as Governor in his own right.

It looked then as though Hoover would have the customary two terms of a successful President. If he did, Franklin would have to be nominated three times for the governorship and could not hope to strike for the Presidency until 1936. His old prophecy that 1932 would be his year seemed less and less likely to come true.

To cut himself off from Smith was to take a considerable risk, but he decided that it was vital to establish an identity of his own. Smith, thinking of Franklin as a protégé who would need his advice, stayed in Albany. But Franklin ignored him and chose very nearly a whole new set of assistants. Sam Rosenman was an exception and so was Frances Perkins. Frances was to become an important co-worker too, and would be with Franklin as long as he lived. But for the most part, he chose new people.

Moreover, Smith soon tired of waiting in an Albany hotel. He left for a job he had taken in New York City; but he was angry. Since Smith was a power in Tammany, his feelings might portend future trouble in party conventions. Franklin's independence might have been bought at too high a price. That remained to be seen.

The Governor's mansion in Albany was to the family just

"The Bosun" and "Meggie" with Eleanor and FDR in Albany,
circa 1930

another of the many homes they had become used to living in. They had Springwood, of course, as a permanent base. Sara still lived there in the old style, although like all other wealthy families, the Roosevelts would be hard hit by the depression. In the Governor's limousine, with outriders of state troopers on roaring motorcycles, there were frequent runs down the Post Road to Hyde Park and back again to Albany.

Eleanor kept house in the mansion in about the same way she always had—by giving orders to servants. There was a steward who was really responsible, so Eleanor could think mostly of the public affairs that had now become an important part of her life. The children were away at school. Their absence gave her freedom to further the welfare causes she cared most about.

The mansion was old but commodious. It had big rooms. overstuffed furniture, large fireplaces, and wide plate-glass windows. It was some distance from Franklin's office; and because of his helplessness, he had to go back and forth by automobile, being lifted in and out and then wheeled up and down specially built ramps. This was, as before, something of a problem. There was always the danger that voters would get the idea that he was helpless in others ways as well. He always had to cope with that possibility.

In the recent campaign he had been frank about his disability. Whenever he appeared, he had been helped to the rostrum, but people who saw it happen, he discovered, tended to forget about it as he threw back his head and began to speak. Smith had helped by saying, when asked whether his protégé's disability extended beyond his legs, that the Governor of New York was not elected to be a circus performer. That remark had circulated widely. Nonetheless, Franklin was always under the compulsion to appear especially vigorous otherwise, and it was sometimes a strain.

His agreeable personality soon had its effect throughout the state. He was a popular Governor. And because he was a recognized party leader, he was frequently consulted by politicians, not only from New York but also from other states. The house at Hyde Park became almost as much a center of political interest as the mansion in Albany. This annoyed his mother, who found it hard to tolerate the characters she often saw and heard conferring with her son. She still thought it would have been more seemly if he had been content to be a quiet country gentleman as his father had been. Eleanor spoke later of this embarrassment:

> She judged people almost solely by their social position, and she continually tried to teach my children to do the same. She found it extremely difficult to get on with Al Smith and many other politicians of the New York City type, and while only people who knew her well could tell when she was being really rude, my children were among those who knew her well. She had the most carrying whisper I have ever heard, and occasionally, during a luncheon at which Franklin was entertaining an important politician, we would all hear her piercing whisper: "Who is that dreadful person sitting next to my son?" Every time there was a big Democratic meeting, her lawn was ruined, and she was miserable about it for days. She was far happier when she could look out her windows and see, resting on the lawn beneath a tree, a guest such as Queen Juliana of the Netherlands [then a Princess]!

"I Remember Hyde Park," *McCall's,* February, 1963.

(10)

THE onset of the Great Depression was a disaster for the nation; but it proved fortunate politically for Franklin. It became apparent, as the months passed and the trouble deepened, that Hoover's inability to cope with it might reduce his chance of re-election. This provided an unexpected opportunity for the Democratic Party—and for Franklin as a potential candidate. The year 1932 again began to seem a magic number.

Hoover did not at first recognize that what had happened was the beginning of a long and wearing ordeal. He did not foresee the increasing numbers of unemployed and the misery of their families. Neither did his advisers or the businessmen and financiers who were so prominent in Republican councils. Consequently what was done to check the decline was always too little and too late.

In past depressions, when the first panic had passed, business activity had picked up slowly at first and then more rapidly; and in a year or two recovery had usually been substantial. Things became much as they had been before the crash. The pattern of former depressions led many people to conclude that recovery was automatic. Consumers had to have houses and clothes and other necessities which had to be grown or made, and this made work on farms and in factories. This was the explanation given for the natural, or automatic, recoveries in the past. It was now being discovered, however, that people might *have* to eat but the system could be so disabled that it could not feed them. Recovery could only come if those who managed affairs made the right moves.

It could soon be seen that the Republicans were making the

wrong moves. Something different from what they were doing was necessary if recovery was to come at all. As Hoover continued to hesitate, Franklin saw what his own attitude should be. It should be just the reverse. He must say definitely that something must be done, and done by the government itself.

Hoover continued to rely on individual action—"rugged individualism"—as the eventual cure. He was averse to federal intervention, and intended to use governmental power only when he felt it absolutely necessary. This was his worst weakness. It would not be true to say that he did nothing. He did a good deal. He was a kind man, and to know that millions of Americans were suffering affected him deeply. But his remedies were not drastic enough for so massive an economic sickness. He recommended— and got passed—a measure to lend relief funds to the states. He started a small public-works program to provide jobs. He set up a Farm Board to buy from farmers the surpluses that glutted the market and depressed the prices of their crops. At his recommendation, the Congress chartered the Reconstruction Finance Corporation to prevent banks and other big businesses from going into bankruptcy. He also appealed to his friends for charity funds to feed and clothe the unemployed and their families.

But some of these remedies did not work—the Farm Board, for instance, was soon swamped by the products it bought to support farm prices. Others were not adequate—loans to the states for relief were far too small, and the public works provided far too few jobs. The calamity was so enormous that it seemed impossible for Hoover's imagination to conceive what vast measures must be taken to check it. Most of what he began would be taken over by Roosevelt and then called "the New Deal." But Roosevelt would be bolder; he would commit the federal government to the responsibilities from which Hoover shrank.

During the awful winter of 1929–30, business did not improve. It grew worse. The charity provided by Hoover and his friends—who continued to be horrified by the thought of the government giving relief—was pitifully inadequate. People waited in soup and bread lines around whole dismal blocks wherever welfare societies operated the kitchens. This disgrace to the proud nation, so recently the leader of the world in production and so willing to proclaim it, was a mystery to everyone. Why did activity not start again?

But it was when the banks began to fail that fright spread like a plague among the more prosperous people. What had been, after all, only a financial panic in 1929 was seen by 1930 to have been the prelude to something far more serious. Business activity slowed down more and more. There were fewer jobs. More and more businesses failed, leaving more and more workers jobless. The emergency measures were, one after the other, overwhelmed by recurring massive events.

One of the worst of these events, and one that had been longest in developing, was the impact on the rest of the economy of a ruined agriculture. During the war in Europe from 1914 until 1918, farmers had been urged to increase production. They had broken new wheatlands to the plow in the short-grass country beyond the Mississippi. They had learned how to grow more corn per acre on farms in the Midwest and more cotton in the South. These staple crops had been needed by nations no longer productive. But when the war ended, the demand for them had lessened. European farmers went back to producing their own crops. This resulted in clogged markets, surpluses held over from year to year, and plunging prices.

This agricultural depression had persisted for almost a decade. Many proposals for doing something about it had been made, but Hoover's Farm Board was the only one accepted by the Republicans. That failed because it proposed only to buy surpluses and sell them abroad—something impossible to do. Foreign countries were reconstructing their own agriculture. They would not admit cheaper American products in competition with their own. American farmers' troubles, thus neglected, spread to the cities both by way of their unpaid debts and their lack of money to buy industrial products.

At Warm Springs, circa 1931

There were other reasons why the Depression was so deep and persistent. One was that the business system tended to shut off its own markets by not allowing workers enough income. When wages were low they could not buy many goods. Owners of business were making profits which were too high, and some of the money which went into profits should have gone to the workers. The owners did not spend all their profits, but tended to save them. They were then invested in speculative ventures in the stock markets—and this helped to account for the feverish boom that had ended in the incredible bust—or they went for some other use *that did not increase industrial activity and expand employment.*

This defect would not cure itself in a system of free enterprise without direction or regulation. When every businessman could do as he pleased, he would do what was most immediately profitable. He did not consider it his duty to pay higher and higher wages as productivity increased. In fact, employers were always fighting to keep wages down, just as workers fought to push them up. Only some sort of government regulation would suffice to establish rules in such matters.

Another problem faced by Hoover was the foreign debt, money owed to the United States by foreign governments and individuals. This vast mass of obligations also resulted from the war. Partly it represented debts incurred in the purchase by the European nations of munitions; partly it represented payments due on investments made abroad by Americans since the war. Economic stagnation had affected other nations even more than it had the United States, and neither public nor private debts could be paid.

The debts had, however, become a political issue. No one dared suggest that they should be canceled. There had been several proposals for reducing those that other governments owed the United States government. But private debts unpaid were as bad as the mass of public debts. Banks unable to collect what was owed to them could not pay what they owed to others—and sometimes they could not even return their depositors' funds. These had been lent to people and businesses who could not pay them back.

All in all, there was a complex of problems, growing more serious for years, that had to be solved before activity would resume. And there was no plan for solving them. That is, there was no plan that was adequate to deal with their complexity and massiveness. Heroic measures were needed. Steps taken by Hoover, however correct in their intention, were wholly inadequate to cope with the deepening disaster.

Perhaps the worst difficulty was that those who had elected Hoover thought that what was happening was like what had happened many times before in our history. They were certain that 1929 was like 1907 and 1893. They refused to believe that there were new and destructive forces at work.

Franklin, as Governor of one of the largest industrial states, discovered somewhat earlier than most responsible public men that recovery was not going to happen unless corrective measures were taken. He did not know what they ought to be. But he was convinced that they could be found. And he did know one thing: the miseries of New York's citizens were intolerable.

He was one of the first to organize public relief and to put into it far more funds than were lent to the state by the federal government. But he learned from this, too, that no state by itself could meet the need. If states competed in devising welfare measures, the most generous of them would go bankrupt. They would attract so many people from other states who needed help that their funds would soon run out.

Franklin's own thinking about recovery did not have to become precise, however, until after another gubernatorial election. (Elections for governor were held every two years until Al Smith's time.) If he should win that, he must offer some real remedies, because then he would inevitably be a candidate for the Presidency. Could his slim victory in 1928 be increased in 1930? If it could, it would show that he had the kind of popular following that impresses delegates to national conventions. Now that the governorship had been forced on him, he had to accept the conditions imposed by this road to the White House: he had to carry his own state by a large majority.

Even before that, he had to be renominated by his own party. He had to calculate now the effect of not having treated Smith with proper respect. The former Governor was still powerful in New York politics; he might well recall the slights of 1928 and influence Tammany to support someone else. But, as it turned out, Smith did not oppose Franklin. The former Governor by now had turned away from politics, having been convinced that the Presidency was quite out of his reach. This conviction would not last: when he saw how favorable a year 1932 was likely to be, he changed his mind and became an active candidate; but in 1930 this had not yet occurred to him.

After his first sharp separation from his predecessor, Franklin had often spoken well of Smith and pictured himself as carrying on in Smith's liberal fashion. This seems to have helped, and since Franklin, as usual, had upstate support, the nomination came to him without contest. It was an election that surprised everyone—including himself: his majority was the largest ever achieved by a gubernatorial candidate up to that time. It was quite obvious after this that he was the front-runner for the Presidential nomination.

He assumed immediately that this was so, and managed his affairs accordingly. Because he was the leading contender, his worst problem was likely to be that all other possible candidates would be active rivals and would combine against him. Following old political custom, they would try to get together and choose one among themselves to support. In this way, they might very well control the convention. This possibility became more likely as the Republican decline went on. Hoover's reputation made it obvious that almost any Democrat could defeat him. Because of this, the nomination was more and more attractive to politicians who thought themselves potential Presidents.

Sure enough, contenders began to appear everywhere. By the beginning of 1932, there were half a dozen who thought they had a chance, among them Governors Ely of Massachusetts and Ritchie of Maryland. There was also Baker of Ohio, who had been Wilson's respected Secretary of War. Most serious of all, however, was the threat of Smith himself, who felt that the party owed him this better opportunity. He now recanted his determination not to run again, and he showed every sign of feeling that he, not Franklin, was the logical designee of the party.

There was one best way to offset Smith's challenge, and Franklin took it. This was to collect enough delegates, pledged in advance of the convention, to win the nomination on the first ballot. This he set out to do. He now had several efficient co-workers besides Howe and Rosenman. Most relied on was James A. Farley, chairman of the state party. It was his job and Howe's to see that delegates designated in state conventions were firmly instructed to vote for Roosevelt at the national convention.

Howe, frail, asthmatic, and morose, stayed in New York and plotted; Farley, large, genial, and outgoing, traveled. He went wherever there was a leader to be persuaded, a delegate to be gained, a primary in prospect, a convention to be held. Franklin ostensibly attended to business in Albany, professing no interest in anything but the job of governing and of doing something for the victims of the worsening Depression.

He did speak of Hoover's ineptitude and of the need for action to oppose the forces bearing down on the small businessmen, and the unemployed. He was vague, but he was emphatic that some action must be taken. The truth was that he knew no more than Hoover what ought to be done. Sam Rosenman persuaded him presently that it was urgently necessary to find out.

Sam was frightened, as everyone was, by the persistence and the effects of the continuing Depression. By the beginning of 1932, there were some thirteen million unemployed; the falling of prices had spread from farm products to manufactured goods, and more and more factories were shut down. Besides this, banks were weakening and many were closing.

A vast, rich, resourceful nation, so recently proud and prosperous, had, in some mysterious fashion, allowed itself to become paralyzed. The business system could not start without some stimulus, and the federal administration could not do anything adequate because of prejudice against governmental action.

Franklin would soon have to state what the remedies should be. It began to seem that nothing less than reconstruction of the whole economy was called for. But for this he felt inadequate. It was more an economic than a political matter. When it was suggested that advice should be sought about the necessary reforms, Franklin quickly agreed. Fortunately there was another helper at hand. This was Raymond Moley, a Columbia University professor. He had been working for Franklin on problems of administration. He was now asked to gather a group of fellow professors who had studied economics and public affairs. Their job was to give advice about ending the Depression.

(**II**)

DURING Franklin's second term as Governor, the Depression had continued to deepen and spread to stable businesses not earlier affected. It was not only the weak enterprises that were failing now, but ones that were long established and reputable. Even old banks were going under. And, of course, the increase in unemployment was frightening.

There was a breakdown in charity because everyone, including the wealthy, suffered from reduced incomes. Worst of all, the public relief agencies, with only small help from the federal government, could not meet the need. The miseries of the winter were heartbreaking for millions of families.

What could be done by one state was discouragingly little. The constitution of New York would not permit borrowing, and when such resources as there were had been used up an already critical situation would turn into disaster. Jesse I. Straus, a successful merchant (Macy's), was made head of a relief agency, with Harry L. Hopkins, a professional social worker, as his assistant. It was as competent an organization as could be found in the country. But its inadequacy only underlined the need for a cure rather than relief, and presently it would have no funds left.

The way to do something substantial for people in misery was to start industrial activity going again. Men able to work needed and wanted jobs. The situation would continue to grow worse until some means for starting activity again were found. And that recovery might not even start until the causes of the trouble had been corrected. There might even be revolution. Such a thing was whispered about by those who had most to lose and were most frightened. The historian Dixon

Wechter described the philosophical implications of these times:

> Too deep for the average citizen to fathom, the floods of dis-
> aster had rolled in to erase the ancient tidemarks and tug at the
> moorings of inherited wisdom. This era brought a questioning
> into American life deeper than any other since the Civil War.
> Stereotypes of thought, traditional saws, the tribal wisdom of
> the elders, all were challenged in books, magazines, and private
> talk. Perhaps, after all, the promise of American life would turn
> out merely to be propaganda. . . .
> An idle man seeking to rationalize his plight was apt to fol-
> low one of several roads. If he saw it as the result of machines
> supplanting men, he might take it all pretty calmly since no one
> could get very angry with a machine. If he blamed himself, or
> his hard luck, he slid down the path of defeat. If he laid the
> responsibility upon society or the economic system, he chose
> the fork of radicalism. The steps of an undetermined number
> veered toward the left. . . . Nearly a quarter of the idle, or about
> four times as many as among the jobholders, agreed that a
> "revolution might be a very good thing for this country."

The Age of the Great Depression, 34.

During the next few months and even on into the campaign, a group of three brought together by Moley acted as
Franklin's advisers, drawing in others as needed. They were
Moley, Adolph Berle, and myself. They discussed among
themselves and with Franklin, during long sessions, what
needed to be done. Gradually his knowledge spread and deepened. After he was elected they continued to work with him,
so that when he assumed office he was ready to take action.
A newsman once spoke of them as "the Brains Trust," and the
name stuck.

Since Franklin's attention must first be given to getting the
nomination, then to being elected, and finally to disposing of
all the political problems a new President must face, what he
would do after he became President must necessarily have a
low priority. Still, some consideration was given to such prob-

Louis Howe, FDR, and James A. Farley, Chicago, 1932

left to right: Admiral Cary T. Grayson, Norman H. Davis, Raymond Moley, the author, William H. Woodin, FDR. On their way to Washington, 1933

lems during the spring. After he was nominated, and then more especially after he was elected, the order of priorities changed. There were some four months after election and before inauguration. Then the President-elect did his hardest thinking and most careful planning. And then the university counselors helped him most.

Nothing had happened to diminish the rich American resources. The productive industrial equipment was still there, even if idle. If fear were first overcome, how could the machine actually be made to work again? First, the Brains Trust felt, by providing cold and hungry people with the means to get shelter and food. Somehow cash must be put into their hands, so that they could buy what they needed. Factories would have to start up to replace what people had bought. People working in factories would be paid and could go on demanding more goods. Thus an upward surge might replace the downward drift of the past few years.

What was necessary then, first of all, they reasoned, was greatly increased relief payments. The government must furnish these either by simply handing out money or by starting up public works to furnish jobs. Franklin favored providing jobs rather than relief money for two reasons. First, he felt that men's pride was involved. They would prefer working for their incomes. But also, there were many jobs to be done that had been long neglected. City streets and country roads could be built or improved; waterworks, power plants, schools, and hospitals were needed. And the national forests and parks were run down and shabby. There was much to be done. Men doing these things would earn pay.

But most of all, they agreed, the people of a nation must see that working for one another and paying one another was the normal state of the economy. And this would happen and go on happening only when their exchanges with one another were substantially equal—when sufficient payment was given for work performed or goods supplied. When, for some reason, the exchange was unequal, those who were underpaid had to restrict their buying; then those who in turn supplied them with goods were without work.

Businessmen had not learned the lesson of such economic equality. Somehow cooperation must be re-established, so that all could prosper together. Reasoning in this way, Franklin arrived at his conclusion. Recovery must begin with an emergency distribution of money to those who had been shut out of jobs or had no source of income. But he began to understand, also, that there must be changes to ensure that large numbers of people should never again be reduced to beggary.

This lesson, worked out in Albany discussions, was the one he expounded during the campaign. He would, he said, accept the responsibility for bringing activities "into concert." Hoover had been reluctant to accept this as a governmental duty. Franklin insisted that it must be done and done vigorously and that it *was* the business of the federal government.

His speeches pursued this theme into many aspects of agriculture, industry, and finance. He showed how the unequal exchanges had come about and how at least some of them could be corrected. He avoided being too specific. A corrective program was something to be worked out carefully; only its general outlines could be seen without intense study. Farmers' incomes must be restored; the families of the unemployed must be given relief and as many as possible put to work; and, gradually, the system must be reformed so that it would not go so wrong again. But this last point was a general promise. It would have to be made specific after he was elected.

The first problem was nomination and election. In this the Brains Trust could not help much; it was mostly a job for the politicians. In the period before the convention Franklin made only a few speeches to underline his general progressive attitudes. He left the maneuvering to Howe and Farley.

By April a simple majority of the delegates had been instructed in state conventions to vote for Franklin; but a two-thirds majority was required to nominate (a convention rule that has since been changed). Somehow many more delegates must be gathered in. Some of these had promised their votes to hopeful candidates from their own states—"favorite sons." Some, from states without primaries, were free and uncommitted. And the coalition headed by Smith, who was now an active contender, was gathering strength. The city bosses who controlled powerful machines—in Kansas City, Boston, New York, and Chicago—were all against Franklin. They swung in behind Smith, the old Tammany favorite, and when the convention began, it looked as though they might very possibly prevent Franklin's nomination.

But what he had counted on did occur. The opposition of Tammany—of bosses Ely in Boston, Hague in Jersey City, Kelly in Chicago, and Pendergast in Kansas City—was what would best persuade the westerners and southerners that he himself was free of machine control. Traditional dislike of Tammany disposed these delegates to accept Tammany's enemies as *their* friends.

It was not actually too difficult then, after preliminary voting had shown where the opposition was, for Farley to make a deal with the westerners who controlled enough votes to make the nomination safe. His proposition to them: If they would vote for Roosevelt, he would accept their candidate for the Vice-Presidency. And so it was arranged in a hectic night of bargaining.

The next day it was done. Smith and the other bosses were defeated. Franklin was chosen on the third ballot, and John N. Garner of Texas was his running mate. The only man who had remained serene throughout the convention was Franklin himself. Now self-assured, used to executive decision, sure of his own power and abilities, he faced the coming campaign with the same confidence he had shown in others. The country was ready for him, he felt, and he was certain he could meet the challenge.

The election proved to be easier than nomination. Franklin need hardly have campaigned at all to have won. Economic conditions, worsening from month to month, discredited Hoover more and more. But thinking of the future and following his usual procedure, Franklin traveled widely and spoke often, offering in this way the alternative to Hoover he intended the voters see.

What he promised was a "New Deal." This he did not define very clearly but it was taken by the unfortunate to mean that their distress would be relieved, and by others to mean that the Republicans, who by now were suspected of having caused the Depression, would be deprived of power. The government, under new leadership, would release the productive forces of the nation. After a few years this could be seen more clearly:

> As we look back through the intervening mists to the campaign of 1932, Franklin can be seen, already larger than life, riding a flood of approval bearing him on to authority far greater even than a President's formal writ. As he stood on election night, when it was all over, high at one end of the huge crowded room in the Biltmore Hotel, Louis Howe on one side, and Jim Farley on the other, the dreams and hopes of all Americans centered in his person. He stood there knowing it, accepting centrality, radiating response; he promised, without saying it, never to abandon his responsibilities; between those who had supported him and the hostile forces they had been learning to dread, he would always intervene. He would do more; he would exorcize the depression and secure them against such dangers in the future as they had just been living through.

The Democratic Roosevelt, 249.

The election won, it now remained to do what had been promised: bring the country out of the Depression and make it secure against such occurrences in the future.

The New Deal was awaited breathlessly.

INAUGURATION day fell on the fourth of March in 1933 (the date has since been changed to January 20). The weather, as usual in Washington at that time of year, was cold and windy. In the morning Franklin rode from the White House up Pennsylvania Avenue to the Capitol with Hoover. On the East Plaza he stood before Chief Justice Stone, his hand on the Dutch family Bible, and repeated the oath of office. Then, his head bare, he made the customary address.

It had been prepared carefully. It contained a rebuke to those, who like the biblical money-changers in the temple, had betrayed the people's trust. This referred to the bankers, who were so thoroughly discredited by recent events. But he also promised aid for those who had suffered most during the months and years just past. The nation must gather its forces and go on, he said, to renewed prosperity. Actually, there was nothing to hold it back except blind, unreasoning fear.

> The only thing we have to fear is fear itself. . . . It is to be hoped that the normal balance of Executive and Legislative authority may be adequate to meet the unprecedented task before us. . . .
>
> But in the event that the Congress shall fail . . . and in the event that the national emergency is still critical, I shall not evade the clear course of duty that will then confront me. I shall ask the Congress for the one remaining instrument to meet the crisis—broad Executive power to wage a war against the emergency, as great as the power that would be given to me if we were in fact invaded by a foreign foe. . . .

Public Papers, 1933, 11.

His words went out by radio to the largest audience, it was estimated, that had ever heard a broadcast. The clear, rich tenor voice spoke to millions whose hopes and fears were deeply involved.

When the ceremony was over, the outgoing President, as was customary, went away alone, and Franklin was driven back to the White House, where he reviewed the inaugural parade from a stand facing Pennsylvania Avenue.

From the number of marching teams, political clubs (Tammany chiefs walked the whole three miles in frock coats and tall silk hats), high-school bands, military detachments, Boy Scouts, state guards (Governor Pinchot of Pennsylvania at the head of his, stood in his car and saluted an old companion as he passed the reviewing stand), no one watching this political pageant could have guessed that the country was in deep trouble. Wave after wave, the marchers came down the broad avenue from the Capitol, afoot, on horseback, in automobiles. They stiffened as they passed the White House; the majorettes stepped a little higher; the bands played their loudest; the cowboys spurred their horses and made them prance.

The President, with his Cabinet, took the marchers' salutes through the long afternoon until darkness had set in. They went then to celebrate a little. They would soon have to see what could be done about the problems they faced.

The Roosevelts, who had their first dinner in the mansion that evening, were better prepared for what was before them than most new Presidential couples are. For one thing, both had often visited the White House during Uncle Ted's administration and again while Franklin had been in Wilson's Navy Department. For four years they had lived in the gubernatorial mansion in Albany, where the social problems were similar.

This familiarity at the start was important, because time was so pressing. Just before inauguration, the failure of banks throughout the country had become epidemic. Depositors' funds had to be saved—such as could be saved—and currency furnished for ordinary transactions. Many of the Democrats who came to the celebration in Washington were without

En route to the Capitol with President Hoover for
FDR's Inauguration, 1933

The first Inauguration, March 4, 1933

ACME PHOTO

With Eleanor and James after the Inauguration, 1933

money to pay their hotel bills, because their funds were in closed banks. There was the same embarrassment everywhere.

This kind of emergency may have been no more than should have been expected, since the economy had ground almost to a stop. As the new Administration began, panic was spreading across the country. It was Franklin's first job to check it. Until he did, he could begin none of the other actions that he had in mind.

Franklin succeeded wonderfully in this. When he had reminded the nation in his inaugural that actually there was nothing to fear but fear itself, people looked at one another and said how true that was. And they began to feel a little comforted. When he said that theirs was a country that recently had been marvelously productive, and that nothing had happened to make it less so, they knew it was true. There were still factories and workmen, still railways and banks. It only remained for things to get going again in different, and fairer, ways—but to get going!

Of course, it was still necessary for Franklin to show the way. People who were hungry must actually be able to buy food; they must have real jobs; factories must run and banks must reopen. The government must see to it that what the businessmen had failed to do by themselves was done with federal aid.

For no better reason than that he sounded confident and promised action, even the business community got back its courage. Hope· replaced despair; yet everyone waited to see what Franklin himself would do. Everyone was ready to cooperate, even those who had voted for Hoover. The unemployed waited eagerly. These were days of breathless anticipation. The first of them wasn't like this; it happened to be a Sunday:

> After he was shaved and dressed, McDuffie, his valet, wheeled him out the long wide corridor and they went down by the lift to the terrace level. Rolling along the flagstones for the first time, he looked out across the lawns at the old trees—and especially the big magnolia he recalled from years before

—and bumping on the stone slabs, came to the office Hoover had left only yesterday. Its curving walls were bare, waiting for his choice of pictures; and when he sat at the large brown desk, his back to the windows, he faced the bareness and shuddered a little; blank walls always annoyed him. There was nothing on the desk but an incoming tray on one side, an outgoing one on the other, a pad with leather corners, a pen set, and a lamp. An empty desk annoyed him too.

McDuffie left and there he was, he used to say, in a bare room, completely alone; there was nothing to be seen and nothing to be heard. The nation, he supposed, was waiting breathlessly for the following up of his brave words of yesterday. There was a financial crisis, activity of all sorts was congealed, and he was expected to find the means for bringing the nation's dying economy back to life. . . . There must be buttons to push, but he couldn't see them. He pulled out a drawer or two. They had been cleaned out.

Presently he sat back in his chair and simply shouted.

The Democratic Roosevelt, 270.

Because he was faced with an immediate emergency, it was important that he had already studied his problems and that he was already an experienced public administrator. He began with the banking crisis. He proclaimed a bank holiday—all banks were closed, some for months, some permanently—but provided an organization to see that solvent institutions rapidly reopened under conditions that assured depositors of the safety of their funds. This required Congressional approval, and he called a special session of the Congress for this purpose. Dixon Wechter chronicled this period:

Action came thick and fast. On Sunday the fifth, Roosevelt called Congress into special session. The next day he forbade the export of gold and all dealings in foreign exchange, and proclaimed a national bank holiday to permit the examination of the soundness of individual banks before their gradual re-opening. . . . On March 9 the Congress of the Hundred Days met to endorse overwhelmingly all the President had done, calling upon the Reconstruction Finance Corporation for new capital to reorganize the banks and authorizing the issue of more currency. . . . In the face of new penalties hoarders began to bring back their gold to deposit windows and turn in their gold certificates. . . . The President serenely went his way. In a broadcast on March 12, the first of what the press called his "fireside chats," he explained in simple words just what had been done, and invited cooperation: "Let us unite in banishing fear" . . . Meanwhile the worst of the crisis had been weathered. Solvent banks began to reopen the next day all over the nation.

The Age of the Great Depression, 66.

There was a firmness about the messages to the Congress, in those earliest days, that carried conviction. And Franklin did not neglect his relations with the millions of people in the country who were waiting so anxiously. He spoke on the radio to vast audiences, telling them that affairs were certainly in a serious state, but also telling them just what he proposed to do. He admitted that much of what would be done was experimental, but said he would watch closely and try something else if the first attempt did not succeed. People listened and approved. White House mail rose to an enormous volume; and congressmen heard from their constituents. There was no doubt that the man who had been elected as an unknown to replace Hoover was by the end of March widely and even enthusiastically approved.

The magic of the Presidency in competent hands consists in this union with the electorate. If leadership is offered in such a way that it carries conviction, it will be accepted. A President with such popular backing as Franklin had in 1933 can for the moment get Congress to do almost anything, however novel, however strongly opposed it may be by those who happen not to like it. This is the honeymoon. It will not last; but while it does, the President can get his way.

Part of the magic, in this instance, came from the majestic Roosevelt presence. Americans are endlessly interested in the Presidency. This includes not only the Chief Executive himself but his family and his associates. This curiosity is satisfied by a large press corps. They record every happening and interview every visitor; they retail volumes of gossip. The Roosevelts were particularly well suited to satisfy this enormous public appetite. Eleanor, who only a few years ago had been a retiring young matron raising a large family under her mother-in-law's sharp scrutiny and living almost as a visitor at Springwood, was now an active partner in the Presidency.

In Washington during Franklin's Navy years, she had been a charming hostess. But so far as anyone knew, she had had no interest in public affairs. The change, so startling to those who did not know her, must always have been latent. It had begun to be evident a long time before, when Franklin was fighting to recover from polio. Sara had aroused Eleanor's resistance by demanding that Franklin return to Hyde Park and gentlemanly pursuits. Eleanor's success in this conflict, with the help of Louis Howe, had encouraged her to develop her public interests.

She and Louis had not liked each other much before this crisis, but working together to bring Franklin around made them firm friends. And what they were able to win gave her a confidence she had never felt before. She never again allowed herself to be dominated by her mother-in-law.

If it was true, as has been said, that Eleanor still carried a certain jealousy of Lucy Mercer, there was no sign of it. That lady was now happily married and living elsewhere. There is some evidence that Franklin saw her occasionally, but they were no more than friendly feelings.

In Albany she had been such an active advocate of all liberal measures that she had become a real, but at that time unnoticed, associate in his political life. She cultivated friends among the active women of the state—for instance, Frances Perkins and Rose Schneidermann, who had helped to develop Franklin's welfare measures.

She approved of the Brains Trust and often joined in their discussions of policy with her husband. She had worked hard during the campaign; and now that she was in the White House, she was an efficient member of its working staff as well as its hostess. The attention she got contrasted startlingly with the modest roles of Grace Coolidge and Lou Hoover, neither of whom had taken any part in public affairs.

She set out to make her husband's administration one that would further all the causes she believed in so deeply—racial equality, protection for women and children, the right of workers to organize, and generous relief measures. She traveled everywhere, and made numerous speeches. She even held press conferences.

Between them, the Roosevelts established a regime that satisfied the American demand for an interesting Presidency. Besides, it was bringing government to bear on many neglected problems. Changes long overdue were now being talked about.

The Roosevelts were a success with the people who had elected them. And for all anyone knew, they were happy together.

(13)

THE first weeks of the Roosevelt Administration are often spoken of as the "Hundred Days." The accomplishments during this time were so astonishing that the allusion to Napoleon's hundred days, his return to Paris from Elba, caught on. The difference, of course, was that Napoleon lost his hundred days' campaign, but Franklin won his. What he asked for, he got. The Congressmen, like the businessmen, were for the moment tamed. It became a perfect honeymoon. The whole country responded:

> What are usually spoken of as "the masses"—meaning large numbers of ordinary uninstructed folk not interested professionally in public affairs and having opinions deriving more largely from impression than consideration—had, by the end of the Hundred Days, accepted Franklin. It would be an exaggeration to say that they understood him. Theirs was not that kind of loyalty. They rather simply had concluded that by and large they had a man in the White House who was for them and against their enemies.

The Democratic Roosevelt, 306.

When the banks' crisis had been alleviated and confidence in them had begun to return, there were other emergency actions to be taken. The highest priority was the economic distress borne by so many families. Franklin asked for funds to be granted—not merely lent—for relief. This was the acceptance of responsibility for the welfare of individuals that he had promised.

To draw unemployment benefits from the U.S. Treasury

still seemed horrifying to most Republicans—and to some Democrats. But this was what the election had been all about. The President was simply carrying out what he regarded as a commitment to those who had elected him.

Having had a competent relief agency in New York, Franklin now appointed one of its executives to manage the new Federal Emergency Relief Administration. This was Harry L. Hopkins, who was to remain a close associate in one job or another as long as Franklin lived. Through the state welfare departments and under the guidance of professional social workers, Hopkins at once began to spread widely and generously the funds appropriated by the Congress.

Franklin had in his mind a plan for a whole system of social insurance. He thought workers ought to contribute, along with their employers, to a fund that would provide for their old age, for disabilities from sickness or accidents, and even for periods of unemployment. But this idea was something he would have to put off for a while. Just now there was an emergency to be dealt with. Relief must be given; but he hoped that public works would soon make it largely unnecessary. He spoke of the emergency in a special message on March 21, 1933:

> It is essential to our recovery program that measures be immediately enacted aimed at unemployment relief. A direct attack on this problem suggests three types of legislation.
>
> The first is the enrollment of workers now by the Federal government for such public employment as can quickly be started.
>
> The second is grants to the States for relief work.
>
> The third extends to a broad public works labor-creating program. . . .
>
> I shall make recommendations to the Congress presently.

Papers, 1933, 80.

There was more optimism than was really justified about these public works. Their usefulness had long been discussed by economists, and some projects had been started by Hoover as the Depression came on. The undertaking had been limited

—not nearly big enough to appreciably affect such an extensive economic sickness. Franklin now asked for an appropriation of more than three billion dollars—an enormous sum in those days—to be used as he directed. He expected to use as much of it as could be spared from direct relief for works projects. Congress, swallowing hard, appropriated the money. The Public Works Administration (PWA) was established, and Harold L. Ickes, Secretary of the Interior, was made administrator.

The immediate results were disappointing. For one thing a good deal of time was required for the planning and designing of such projects as dams, waterworks, parks, power plants, public buildings, and river and harbor improvements. Jobs were not quickly forthcoming.

As soon as this became apparent, Harry Hopkins was authorized to set up the Civil Works Administration (CWA) to look for and carry out projects that required little preparation and no heavy materials, so that they could be started at once. He called on local officials everywhere to find out what needed to be done locally. Such projects could give jobs immediately —repairing streets, cleaning up parks in the cities, building small dams and making dirt roads in the country—all to be paid for by the federal government. The CWA was supplanted presently by the better organized Works Progress Administration (WPA).

Franklin's plan for the federal government to enroll workers started poorly, but soon was going well. As fears were quieted and confidence restored, however, criticism of Franklin's programs sprang up. In fact, the rise of belligerent opposition to the New Deal was amazingly quick to follow the first signs of recovery.

Conservatives suddenly seemed a little ashamed of their recent meekness. They had ample opportunity to express themselves since they owned most of the newspapers and radio stations. Before long, even by the fall of 1933, a lively campaign of opposition to all the New Deal undertakings had materialized. Hopkins remained for years a favorite target.

The CWA and WPA were vulnerable to ridicule because

many of the projects were not really necessary and also because they were not carried out very efficiently. Unless allowance were made for the half-starved condition of the workers to begin with, it was easy to criticize their poor performance. "Leaf raking" became a byword and a good deal of bitter humor was used on starved men who seemed to lean on their tools more often than they used them. What was also ignored was a fact as apparent to critics as to anyone else. Getting projects finished was only a secondary purpose. The first consideration was to give men earnings that they could take home to their families.

Other New Deal projects were begun almost at once. Some were well received, and some were not. But whether they were or not depended more on the attitude from which they were viewed than on the results they achieved. Franklin, being experienced in government, anticipated opposition. But as soon as he found that the Congress was in a pliant mood—reflecting the country's approval—he decided to take advantage of this cooperativeness and propose some other schemes that might otherwise have been postponed.

Several of these were novel, as Franklin readily admitted in a March 19, 1933, farm proposal:

> Deep study and counsel of many points of view have produced a measure which offers great promise of good results. I tell you frankly that it is a new and untrod path, but I tell you with equal frankness that an unprecedented condition calls for the trial of new means to rescue agriculture. If a fair administrative trial of it is made and it does not produce the hoped for results I shall be the first to acknowledge it and advise you.

Papers, 1933, 74.

One of these "new means" had to do with agriculture, one with industry, and several with government credit.

The credit measures were intended to assist those who were losing farms, homes, or businesses because as things were they could not pay their debts. The Farm Credit Administration, a Home Owners' Loan Corporation, and an enlargement of the Reconstruction Finance Corporation were all quickly authorized. The Reconstruction Finance Corporation had been in existence for some time and had recently made large loans to banks, insurance companies, and railroads. It was now to extend its services, helping many businesses to regain their solvency and go on with their operations. The Home Owners' Loan Corporation extended credit to people all over the country who could not meet their mortgage payments. It saved them from being put out on the streets. Practically all of them could meet their obligations when recovery got under way.

The thorough reorganization of the agricultural credit system did for farmers what the Home Owners' Loan Corporation did for those who would otherwise have lost their homes. It saved their farms. But, of course, it did far more than that. It was intended to be—and was—a permanent assistance to farmers, helping them not only to carry their debts for land, but to borrow for the purchase of machinery, cattle, and seed.

But of all the New Deal agencies, the most novel and far-reaching were the Agricultural Adjustment Administration (AAA) and the National Recovery Administration (NRA). Both were established by laws passed during the hundred days.

These were not only novel, they were controversial. Neither survived long in its original form; but this was for different reasons. The AAA, after a year of operation, was declared unconstitutional by the Supreme Court for what amounted to a technical reason; and farm relief had to take another form. The NRA was struck down by the Court even sooner because, the Court said, it delegated powers to the President that the Congress must reserve to itself. It was never revived.

Since these agencies were so prominent in the New Deal scheme, we must look briefly at each of them.

(**14**)

DURING World War I, as previously noted, many farmers had been urged to grow more crops because the Allies needed them, and they had responded by buying land and expanding their operations. For this purpose they had borrowed heavily. To get a loan, a farmer had to mortgage his property. This meant giving the bank he borrowed from the right to take over his property if he could not pay back the loan. He also had to pay interest. He had expected to pay the interest and installments on the loan out of his returns from the sale of his corn, wheat, soybean, hogs, or whatever he produced. For a while he had been able to, because prices in wartime were high and the demand for his products was urgent.

After the war, however, the demand had decreased, especially from foreign markets, and prices had fallen drastically. But mortgage and interest payments remained as high as ever. Farmers simply could not sell their produce for enough to pay what they owed the banks. It was even hard for them to meet family expenses. What could they do? For millions of farmers there was no choice. They lost their farms; the mortgages were foreclosed.

Like the factory workers who had been doing war work, they found themselves among the unemployed. Some hung on somehow, using up all their savings, borrowing, perhaps, from more fortunate relatives, and hoped for a change. But they were bitterly certain that they were being unfairly treated. Demand for factory products soon recovered, but not that for farm products. When farmers could not buy manufactured items, factories could not sell as much and trouble that had begun in agriculture gradually spread to industry. Franklin explained this simply in a July, 1933, "Fireside Chat":

> If all of our people have work and fair wages and fair profits, they can buy the products of their neighbors and business is good. But if you take away the profits of half of them, business is only half as good. It does not help much if the fortunate half is very prosperous; the best way is for everybody to be reasonably prosperous.

Papers, 1933, 297.

By 1929 the banks were in difficulty, too. The loans they had made to farmers were not being paid back. If the banks seized the farms, they could not sell them to anyone else; so this would not get back the money belonging to the bank's depositors. Since many depositors were losing *their* jobs, they could not buy the products of the factories. Factories were therefore forced to close down because they could not sell *their* products: Thus many *more* people lost their jobs. It was a cycle of distress. It seemed unfair to everyone caught in it.

This was "deflation," something Americans had experienced before. Actually what this word meant was that more could be bought for a dollar than could be bought before—if you had the dollar. At the same time it meant that if you were selling something, you got fewer dollars than before for what you sold. This was what was happening to the farmers. They got fewer dollars for their cattle and hogs, for instance, but they had to pay the same number of dollars on their debts.

Farmers might be—they were—the most conservative of all Americans; but after ten years of being squeezed in this way, they were in a revolutionary mood. Some were taking direct action. Neighbors were getting together and preventing the banks from foreclosing by threatening potential buyers. Sometimes they even used force against auctioneers sent by the courts to sell their farms.

All during the years since 1921, there had been agitation for some kind of relief. In this, as in other affairs, the Republicans in power had been reluctant to allow government inter-ference. It was still felt that if the situation were left alone, it would somehow right itself. Markets would recover, prices would rise, jobs would increase, debts would be paid, and prosperity would return to the farms. But this did not happen. By 1933 there were enormous surpluses of agricultural prod-ucts that could not be sold or were sold at extremely low prices, and farmers could not buy the manufactured goods they needed, let alone pay their debts, or even interest on them.

It seemed to Franklin from the beginning that the burden of debt must be lightened; some means must be found to raise the level of agricultural prices so that the farmers' debts *could* be paid. One of the first steps in any such effort would be to make it impossible for international speculators dealing in gold to bid its price up any further and so to push down the price of goods. For this reason the export of gold was pro-hibited. This, Franklin thought, ought to have the immediate effect of giving farmers more income. At an April 19, 1933, press conference, he told the nation:

> If I were going to write a story, I would write it along the lines of the decision that was actually taken last Saturday, but which goes into effect today, by which the government will not allow the exporting of gold. . . .
>
> The whole problem before us is to raise commodity prices. For the last year the dollar has been shooting up and we de-cided to quit competition. The general effect will probably be an increase in commodity prices. . . .
>
> We have got to come back to a recent level, but not to the 1929 level except in certain instances. City real estate then was altogether too high . . . and ought not to be brought back to that level. . . . On the other hand farm prices were com-paratively low in 1929 and have been going down steadily. . . . So it has got to be a definitely controlled inflation. . . .

Papers, 1933, 139.

There were various other proposals. In fact there were so many and disputes about them were so difficult that the Democrats in the Congress despaired of finding any plan that would be supported by a majority.

Even before his election, Franklin and those working with him were well aware of the difficulty of solving the farm problem. It was a complex and explosive issue. It had become more controversial as time passed. But anyone running for the Presidency would have to say something about it.

What he did was to tell the quarreling farm groups that they must get together and work out an agreement. Only if they did that would he ask the Congress to enact the necessary legislation. Since something must be done quickly, the holdover Congress was asked to pass an act allowing any one of several remedies to be used. The act was submitted but it failed to pass before Franklin took office. Another version was submitted after he became President and late in the spring it was passed. It authorized several different schemes for the Secretary of Agriculture to choose among. What the Brains Trust favored was a scheme called the "domestic allotment plan." This would permit farmers growing wheat, cotton, and corn to plant a total of only as much of these products as was consumed at home in the United States in normal years. Others favored an attempt to sell large amounts of these products to foreign countries at less than cost, with the federal government making up the difference in order to give the farmer a profit. This was called "dumping." It was what Hoover's Farm Board had tried to do but without success. Another scheme was to put the responsibility on the processors of food products—those who made flour out of wheat, for instance—to pay profitable prices to farmers and pass on the higher prices to consumers.

The bill that passed actually included all three schemes. But Secretary of Agriculture Wallace, who was given the responsibility for putting this Agricultural Adjustment Act into operation, relied mostly on the domestic allotment device. He had been persuaded that it was the most likely to succeed.

This plan called for committees of farmers to be set up in each county. They would be told by the Department of Agriculture how many acres of each crop should be planted. The committees would then tell each individual farmer how many of his acres he might use to grow each of the products in the plan. In return for cooperating in this way, he would be compensated for the acres he allowed to be idle.

Each farmer's allotment of acreage depended upon how many acres he had used in previous years to grow these crops, so that a fair division among the farmers in each county could be made. The total of allotments throughout the country was calculated to produce what would be used in a normal year and paid for at a fair price.

This fair price—normal year standard—was called "parity," and it was intended to equalize farm and industrial incomes. When this happened, farmers would be able to buy manufactured goods, and manufacturers would be able to buy farm products. By such an equal exchange each great sector of the economy would be stabilized and could keep going.

To pay farmers for cooperating, a processing tax was provided. This was a tax on the milling of wheat into flour, the making of cotton into cloth, and the butchering of hogs. This tax money was to be used to compensate farmers for the land they left idle in order to reduce surpluses. Although it was understood that the tax would raise prices to consumers—since the tax would be added to retail prices—the theory was that if unemployment were eliminated and people's incomes increased, people would be able to pay more for these products, and farmers would then have incomes and would again be customers for factory goods.

Officials capable of managing the Agricultural Adjustment Administration had to be found, and offices had to be set up. The need was so great that experts from all over the country were persuaded to assist. Soon the processing taxes were being collected and checks were going out to farmers. It was a tremendous job of organization and cooperation, carried out efficiently.

It was not long before there was criticism of this venture, as of other New Deal agencies. To the critics it seemed ridiculous to pay farmers for *not* planting crops. They pointed out that the production of food was being limited at a time when many people were hungry. They did not listen when the answer was made that the staple crops existed in huge surpluses at giveaway prices—and still were not in demand. Even if the nation had been prosperous, wheat and cotton in the quantities being produced would not be used or needed. What *was* needed was meat, dairy products, and other protein foods, and the production of these was being encouraged, not limited.

The program was popular with the farmers, however, who understood from hard experience how important the parity concept was. They cooperated fully.

The loudest criticism arose when the future crop of hogs was reduced by destroying little pigs. The wailing of the opposition newspapers about this was loud and long. It was only partially checked by a reminder to city editors by a newspaper editor in Iowa—a corn-hog state. Little pigs, he told them, were not, after all, raised to be pets. What was so bad about slaughtering them when small if they were to be slaughtered anyway when they were big?

Secretary Wallace and the Administration did not succeed very well in educating the public to the economic necessity of bringing farmers back into the same exchange relationship with industrial workers that had once existed. Then everyone had prospered. Nevertheless, the agricultural program did continue and did have the desired equalizing effect.

(**15**)

WHEN the farmers' problems had thus been tackled, the President turned his attention to industry. He asked the Congress to pass a National Industrial Recovery Act, planned to do for manufacturers what the Agricultural Adjustment Act was doing for farmers. Many people had ideas about what should be done to get activity started in industry, and Franklin had listened to many suggestions without being able to decide just what ought to be done. He was inclined to follow the same procedure he had used with the farm leaders —insist that the promoters of various plans get together and work out something they could agree to try. If they would do this he felt the concerted effort might result in starting a recovery.

For some years trade associations had been developing. Franklin had, in fact, been interested in one of them as a lawyer—the Construction Council. He had argued for it with the then Secretary of Commerce—Hoover. So it was natural that he should again think of such organizations as a possible way of bringing about the cooperation he hoped for.

These associations were intended to prevent unfair competition. A furniture manufacturer, for instance, who paid lower wages and used cheaper materials than other furniture manufacturers, would have lower costs and so could undersell his competitors. He might, in fact, force his competitors to adopt the same practices or to go out of business. The manufacturers in many industries had therefore banded together in an effort to prevent their less ethical members from forcing all of them to lower their standards. But these associations had not been successful because they had found no way of disciplining those who refused to cooperate.

The NRA proposed to legitimize these industry organizations and provide the discipline they had been unable to impose on themselves. The procedure was to make up a code of fair practices for each trade and require all members to comply with it or lose their membership or, perhaps, their license to do business. Thus ethical businessmen would be protected from less scrupulous competitors, consumers would be assured of quality products, and, it was hoped, workers would be treated more fairly than they had been in the past.

Labor organizations saw in this arrangement the possibility of making gains they had long hoped for. The codes could well provide that paying wages below a certain level was an unfair practice. Collective bargaining—negotiation between employers and union officials speaking for the employees— also was something labor desperately wanted and something employers had fought against. It, too, might be legitimized by being written into industry codes.

There were other gains to be had. For instance, child labor, still disgracefully prevalent in textile mills, could be forbidden. Reforms of this kind appealed not only to other manufacturers who disliked such practices but to liberals of all sorts. The Brains Trust saw in the NRA the possibility of more orderly planning for production. Industries could do the planning in regularly held conferences with government representatives supervising the process and making sure that the public was protected. Materials and money could be used more efficiently; waste could be reduced by making sure that no capital was invested worthlessly.

After many conferences with representatives of business and industry and many amendments, all these provisions were finally written into one comprehensive law, which was passed on June 16, 1933, much to Franklin's gratification:

The law I have just signed [he said] was passed to put people back to work, to let them buy more of the products of farms and factories and start our business at a living rate again.

In my Inaugural I laid down the simple proposition that nobody is going to starve in this country. It seems to me to be equally plain that no business which depends for its existence on paying less than living wages has any right to continue. . . . The change can be made by an industrial covenant to which all employers shall subscribe.

. . . No employers, and no group of less than all employers in a single trade could do this alone. But if *all* employers in each trade now bind themselves faithfully in these modern guilds— without exception—and agree to act together and at once, none will be hurt and millions of workers, so long deprived of the right to earn their bread in the sweat of their labor, can raise their heads again.

Papers, 1933, 251.

As soon as the bill was passed an administration was set up to carry out its provisions. General Hugh Johnson was named as administrator. When conferences to write codes were called, the businessmen involved did make concessions to labor, because the time had come when they must. They were not anxious, however, to make concessions that would benefit consumers. In fact, as finally written under General Johnson's supervision, most of the codes had provisions against reducing prices. Agreements of that kind had always been forbidden by the antitrust laws.

Johnson defended these concessions because he felt that codes with such provisions were better than indefinite delays or no codes at all—which would have been the alternatives. The President was persuaded to approve them for much the same reason. But they offended many progressives, and it was obvious from the beginning that the NRA would have a hard time surviving.

These were the acts of the Hundred Days that seemed most significant and attracted most attention. But there were others as well, some hardly less important.

There was, for instance the law establishing the CCC

(Civilian Conservation Corps). Franklin valued this effort highly because it combined (as, of course, public works did too) unemployment relief and the building of much needed public improvements. It provided for setting up camps for young men whose families were destitute, who could therefore not go on with their education, and who could find no jobs. These young men were paid, but not a full wage, because they were being furnished a living under exceptional circumstances and also being started in education. No boy need join if he did not want to, but many thousands did. They worked in the national and state forests and parks, planting and cultivating trees, improving recreational areas, building campgrounds and cabins, and making roads and trails. It proved one of the most popular of all the New Deal programs.

Comparable with this was another vast project for bringing under control a whole river system—the Tennessee. Dams were to be built to provide electric power for industry; and these same dams, by controlling floods, would stop an almost yearly disaster along the Ohio River. Also, to protect reservoirs, the surrounding hills would be reforested and vast areas opened for recreation and eventually for the production of timber. The Tennessee River had first been dammed during World War I to furnish power for fertilizer production. Since then Senator Norris of Nebraska and other progressives had been trying to persuade the Congress that such governmental development of this river system ought to be extended. There were others who wanted to turn the existing dam over to private business, and the controversy had caused heated debate for years. The progressive veterans were delighted with Franklin's decision to sponsor the Authority, and it was approved by the Congress without difficulty.

While the Agricultural Adjustment, the National Recovery and Public Administrations, the Civilian Conservation Corps, and the Tennessee Valley Authority were getting under way, the new relief and credit agencies provided emergency assistance. The extension of credit—making it possible to borrow money at low interest rates—saved people's homes and businesses while relief payments were enabling them to pay rent and buy food.

But the numbers of the unemployed were still nearly as large as ever before and Franklin felt that something more drastic would have to be done. At this point he and General Johnson conceived the Re-employment Agreements. This was a venture that appealed to Franklin's lively spirit; and it was a way of meeting the crisis which, he felt, would stir businessmen out of their lethargy and induce them to enlarge their enterprises. It was undertaken with tremendous promotional commotion and for a few weeks it seemed effective in starting the paralyzed economy going again.

The idea was that if all employers would agree at once to re-employ their workers at fair wages, members of the whole system of business who followed this practice would buy and sell to each other. Demand and supply would be created together. And with such a start everyone would be able, with the wages he got, to buy what was made by others.

As a first inducement, the NRA would allow those who complied to display the Blue Eagle. This was to be the badge of cooperation. Those who could not display it in their store windows or on the walls of their offices would be marked as unpatriotic. There was, in fact, a rush to get Blue Eagles. But it was too easy to get them without really complying; and there were so many chiselers that the whole intention was defeated.

As the Blue Eagle was discredited, criticism of the other agencies tended to rise, too. By late fall of 1933, it was evident that something drastic would again have to be undertaken.

(16)

THE prospect of winter in the fall of 1933 was not really so dismal as it had been the year before. Even for the unemployed, there was an allowance to buy groceries and the rent could be met. This was about all that could be done with meager relief allowances, but it was better than nothing. Roosevelt proclaimed the new optimism in his Thanksgiving day proclamation:

> May we be grateful for the passing of dark days; for the new spirit of dependence one on another; for the closer unity of all parts of our wide land; for the greater friendship between employers and those who toil; for a clearer knowledge by all nations that we seek no conquests and ask only honorable engagements by all peoples to respect the lands and rights of their neighbors; for the brighter day which we can win by seeking the help of God in a more unselfish striving for the common betterment of mankind.

Papers, 1933, 495.

Actually, except for this temporary help, people's prospects were not much better than before. Public works were dreadfully slow in getting started; prices of food had risen because of the processing taxes going to the farmers, so consumers often could not buy what was needed; and unemployment was only a little reduced from its high level of the spring because industry simply stayed in a state of suspension. When Franklin tried to measure the total effect of the new government agencies, he had to admit that it was nothing remarkable. But if he was disappointed no one knew it. He was giving an incredible exhibition of persuading people that they were better off than they actually were.

But he was not one to fool himself. He looked on the nation, and all that went on in it, as his responsibility. He had none of the stand-offish attitude of those Presidents—a long line of them—who had merely presided passively over a government not really expected to do much of anything except when the national security was threatened.

It was this difference in attitude, more than any specific action, that made people willing to wait patiently even if they were not much better off. Franklin intended to see that people were more certain of their jobs—if not good jobs, still ones that gave them something to do. And they could be assured that some emergency measure would provide them and their families with absolute necessities.

No one had expected this of government before this depression. In previous years, the first concern of officials, and especially of Presidents, had been to assist businessmen in every way possible, mostly by helping them to make money. If they were prosperous, part of their prosperity would trickle down to others—Andrew Mellon, Secretary of the Treasury in the Harding and Coolidge Cabinets, had put it just that way. When profits were high, all was well, satisfied employers would provide jobs and workers should be grateful. They should also be content with such wages as employers felt they could afford.

This was the fallacy of the boom years. Looking back from the Wall Street crash of 1929, it could be seen that during the ten years preceding, *real* wages (that is, what a day's pay would buy) had in fact fallen. Businessmen did furnish jobs; but the jobs did not pay well enough to make good customers out of workers. There was a tremendous boom in securities; speculation was wild in real estate; and many paper fortunes were made overnight. But after ten years of the New Era (as its beneficiaries liked to call it) most people were not much better off than they had been at the beginning. Prosperity had *not* trickled down.

But now Franklin meant to reverse the rule—a living for the many would come first; business prosperity must come from providing that living to satisfied consumers.

Free enterprise would have to stop short of freedom to exploit labor and consumers. It was now noted by skeptics that free enterprise had never really existed anyway. Competition, the supposed regulator, was largely a myth. Monopolies had taken over huge sectors of the economy. Workers in the employ of these giants had no alternatives. It was not easy to find other jobs when they left the ones they had; and when they were underpaid and overworked, as they often were, all they could do was to give in or to strike; and a strike at that time was often fearfully like a civil war. The police were instructed to protect property, and often they were required to protect strikebreakers. After all the strife and sacrifice, what workers gained was usually very little. On the whole the gains they made were not enough to sustain an economy that depended on consumers buying goods from farm and factory.

Consumers had no alternative either. They could pay what was asked for goods or they could do without. They were persuaded by advertisers to commit themselves to paying in installments for more goods than they could afford. But nothing could be more certain than the inevitable result. If consumers' debts grew beyond their ability to pay, a reckoning would surely come. It had come for millions in 1929.

Franklin said, in a thoughtful moment, when he had had some experience as President, that he had to be more a teacher than anything else. And every day in some way he did try to do a little teaching. He told the bankers that they must stop using their depositors' funds for speculation; this was one reason many banks had been unable to meet the demands upon them for cash in the crisis. He told businessmen that they must treat workers as potential customers; this was only fair; and they must be bargained with to make the fairness apparent. He told workers they had a duty to their families and the community along with the rights they were so indignantly demanding. And his preachment to the whole nation was that everyone was responsible for everyone else, that all must work together, trying more to help than to get the best of bargains. This was in harmony with the Christian doctrine he had learned from his father, from Peabody at Groton, and had heard often in his church.

The strange thing about this is that Hoover was a good Christian too. He was of the Quaker sect; and he had labored mightily to rescue European masses from starvation. If there ever was a Good Samaritan on a grand scale it was Hoover on his mission to a continent devastated by World War I. The contrast between the two was that Franklin's Christian philosophy extended to making the economic system fair to all. In the modern world, he believed, charity is not enough; and good works are not enough. Out of the system must come fair wages, fair prices, honest goods and services. And government must be vigilant to do its part.

Franklin was not a sermonizer. He was inclined to be gay. His laugh could often be heard ringing through the White House. His press conferences and fireside chats were both informative and hopeful.

The old mansion overflowed with company and good cheer. The Roosevelt entertainments were enormous and included all sorts of people. Their Sunday suppers—when Eleanor demonstrated proudly that she had at least learned to scramble eggs in a chafing dish—were occasions that enlarged their circle of friends. In his velvet dinner jacket, the President was the perfect father figure. He was the center of attention for the whole table and he allowed himself to seem indiscreet about what was going on, so that visitors were sure they were sharing state secrets.

Franklin still went to Warm Springs. He had known before he left there in the fall of 1928 to run for Governor of New York that there was no hope of regaining the use of his legs. But he had gone back when he could while he was Governor and continued his visits now that he was President. It was a place that gave him peace.

It had become a tradition at the Springs that the President

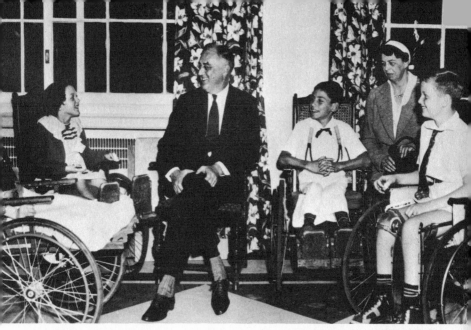

With a group of young patients in Warm Springs, 1938

Harry L. Hopkins, FDR, and Mrs. Roosevelt leaving Warm Springs for Washington, 1938

would always be there to carve the Thanksgiving turkey in the big dining room of Georgia Hall; and in spring, when the first azalias bloomed, he was certain to show up. It was a large institution now. An annual fund-raising drive called the "March of Dimes," managed by his old-time law partner, Basil O'Connor, had furnished the funds to make it the first complete polio rehabilitation center. Happily these funds were sufficient to support similar centers in other places too.

Franklin had built himself a small colonial-style cottage too, some way up the mountain from the hospital. Until now he had lived in rented houses when he went there. In this very year of 1933 he occupied his cottage for the first time, and, inevitably it was called the Little White House. There were times when it became almost as famous as the big one in Washington.

At Thanksgiving time in 1933, when the special railway car he used, the Magellan, carried him down to West Georgia, he was not satisfied; but he felt he had done all he could. A trainload of newspapermen went with him and scattered out through the small community to tell the nation in daily dispatches all that went on among patients and visitors. These doings included not only the traditional dinner in Georgia Hall but evenings at nearby places such as the Calloway estate, picnics on the banks of the Flint River, and barbecues with Mayor Allcorn and other neighbors.

Franklin was no esthete; he was no littérateur; he did not know good music from bad; but the pleasure he got from country singing with everyone joining in the choruses was so obvious that everyone around enjoyed it with him. He exercised with other patients in the big new pool, drove about the countryside, and had a little time to read or sit on his new porch in the sun.

Eleanor was not so fond of the Springs. Georgians got on her nerves and she on theirs. They were critical of her liberal views and especially her refusal to tell black from white in a person's skin. And she was not fond of farms and woods as

Franklin was. When she could not avoid a visit, she at least cut her stay very short.

Franklin had many visitors, some invited and some not. It was part of his existence that wherever he went he had to take everything and everybody pertaining to the Presidency with him. The government was where he was. And a press conference under the pines in West Georgia carried just as far across the country as did one in the White House. If, ten minutes later, the reporters were joining his family of associates in bawling "Home on the Range" and picnicking on Brunswick stew in a clearing along the river, it all helped to convey to the nation that there was a big, healthy man in charge who meant to get a lot done before he was through.

(**17**)

OPPOSITION to most of the New Deal undertakings continued to grow. The critics were not in the majority, obviously, but they could make themselves heard. Businessmen, and especially the financial fraternity, were worried about Franklin's intentions. They were afraid that recovery would not restore the conditions they had profited from in other days. And they were right. Things would never be the same again.

Employers did not easily make all the concessions to labor demanded of them; the processors of farm products objected strongly to any limitation of production that would reduce the volume passing through their factories; and the whole financial community disliked the extending of credit by the government (through the new Farm Credit system and the Home Owners' Loan Corporation), and feared the reforms they could see coming.

Newspapers and radio stations, owned by people who were businessmen themselves, were against the reforms. As the businessmen began to get back on their feet they began to carp and deplore. At first this was mostly talk among themselves; but soon it began to appear in the press and be heard over the air. It increased in volume until finally it became a prolonged complaint which lasted all through Franklin's administrations. The New Deal, newspapers and radio stations said, was radical; it was even—horrid word—"red." Franklin himself was not attacked for some time, although this too would come. In the early years, he was too popular. It was his associates who were blamed.

But newspapers and radio commentators were trying to stem a wave of support that would not be contained. As the

Hearst, Gannett, and Scripps-Howard papers, one after another, turned first against Franklin's associates and then against Franklin himself, they failed to convince their readers. It was well known that the reporters in Washington did not agree with their publishers' views, and Franklin was shrewd enough to take advantage of this. He held regular press conferences, often took newsmen into his confidence, and generally treated them as friends. So, even though the editorial pages were more and more hostile, the news from the White House continued to be reported. And since even hostile publishers could not still the insatiable curiosity about the President, there was excellent coverage. People became cynical about the slanted news and critical comments. Because the White House was open to reporters, because Franklin was always doing something to be watched or inventing something to be written about, and because anything the lively Roosevelt family did was news, the intimacy between the President and the people could not be stifled. Old-timers recalled that it had been much the same when Uncle Ted had been President. He, too, had been unpredictable, disliked by conservatives, distrusted by business, but tremendously active in keeping the country informed. The difference was that in Franklin's day the methods of communication were more far-reaching, and more of the people quickly came to know—and approve—of what he did.

It began to seem that Franklin could not be touched by criticism; people would not have it. The editorialists and the excited reactionaries on the radio may as well have saved their effort and their breath. The New Deal was approved. The newspaper campaign may even have served to confirm the general belief that Franklin was the friend of the people, not of those who had got the nation into trouble when they had been in power.

During Franklin's first years, newspaper and radio opposition concentrated particularly on the Brains Trust. It was pictured as responsible for every move and every measure the businessmen objected to.

The professors, it was said, had invented the new agencies that were being set up so freely; they were "theorists" and impractical; and, finally, none of them "had ever met a payroll." All this was somewhat irrelevant because, actually, the Brains Trust no longer existed. It had been useful during the campaign and throughout the interlude before inauguration; but when Franklin moved into the White House he at once had an official family of Cabinet members and secretaries much more numerous and varied in experience than the few professors he had relied on before. Members of the original group were either minor officials now, or had gone back to their former occupations.

Raymond Moley, for example, who had been the organizer, left within a year to go back to his Columbia professorship and to journalism. Others who took on emergency jobs in the Administration inherited the name even though they were quite different from the old academic group, and even though they had very different ideas. The Brains Trust lingered on in the propaganda of the opposition but not in actuality.

Besides, despite their position of whipping boys for the press, the Brains Trust members, by late 1934, had begun to lose their influence with Roosevelt. Their place was taken by a group whose major spokesman was Felix Frankfurter, then a professor at Harvard and often a visitor at the White House. He spoke for an old-fashioned progressivism whose oracle was Justice Brandeis of the Supreme Court. To understand Franklin's change, it is necessary to look at what the progressives thought, and why.

With the great advances in technical knowledge around the turn of the century, it became possible to use machines for much of the work formerly done by men's hands and muscles. The result was that fewer employees were needed. This meant first, that the owners of large industries became very wealthy and, consequently, very powerful; and second, that many laboring men could no longer get work at decent wages because so many of them were no longer needed. This latter condition was made worse by the waves of immigrants coming to the United States from Europe willing to work for low wages and under miserable conditions because even these were an improvement over those in their homelands.

Great fortunes were being made by a relatively few men who gained control of entire industries either by forcing their competitors out of business or buying them out. They were then free to dominate large sectors of the American economy. Government regulation was ineffective because it was held that if business was left "free," eventually, through competition, prices would become reasonable and employers would be forced to pay decent wages.

The progressives, however, believed that these monopolies and "trusts," rather than leading to free competition, actually prevented competition through control of prices and wages. Uncle Ted had been a progressive, at least during his Bull Moose Campaign in 1912, and in 1934 there were many progressives in the Congress—such respected figures as Senators Norris of Nebraska, Johnson of California, Wheeler of Montana, and La Follette of Wisconsin. It was their position that the free enterprise system could only operate to bring about the desired results if monopolies were broken up or prevented from forming. If one firm controlled all aspects of an industry, they reasoned, no competition would develop; but if many firms were active in that industry, competition among them for buyers would ensure fair prices and decent wages.

The older progressives argued that the "collectivism" represented by NRA was the wrong way to establish economic justice, and they urged Roosevelt to go back to the enforcement of free enterprise. When the Blue Eagle campaign bogged down, and when businessmen began to oppose the Administration for being "radical" (although in effect the NRA was their own creature) Brandeis and Frankfurter felt they were presented with an opportunity.

These issues were fought out within the Administration, although the public knew little about the struggle. Franklin never mentioned it, and its general meaning was difficult for reporters to explain. All the public knew was that Franklin was attacking his problems vigorously, first in one way and then in another.

The collectivists fought a losing battle around Franklin's desk. The beginning of the end for them was represented by the arrival in Washington of Thomas Corcoran and Benjamin Cohen, recent students of Frankfurter, toward the end of 1934. The President accepted them as assistants and soon they had placed in government agencies dozens of others who agreed with them. Most of them being lawyers, they were able not only to assist in drafting many new laws but to influence their administration. Since the progressives now far outnumbered the collectivists and, more important, had the support of the President, the remaining members of the Brains Trust soon resigned.

By that time Franklin recognized that NRA as it was being administered was a failure. When, on May 27, 1935, the Supreme Court declared that the Congress had delegated more powers than the Constitution allowed, Franklin did not try to re-establish it. What historians speak of as the first New Deal was over. The second New Deal had started. Franklin continued to experiment, seeking answers to the problems of the lingering depression.

Franklin did on occasion, as he was considering a problem, talk with those around him rather as though he was thinking out loud. But he came to his own conclusions without saying what it was he was trying to do . . . and he would never admit that any change had taken place. Even his thinking out loud was usually a justifying soliloquy. He was merely pursuing his experimental way toward recovery and reform. . . .

The result was the shaping of those policies which came to be called the second New Deal, the kind of thing the old gentlemen on the Supreme Court approved. Relief could be given, welfare measures could be enlarged, public works could be undertaken; but he must abandon his leaning toward collectivism. He must support free enterprise and keep the government out of it.

The Democratic Roosevelt, 328.

The second New Deal, then, after Franklin realized that he could not get acceptance for the collectivist approach to national economic problems, was a return to more traditional policies. During 1935 there would be stringent acts to control banking and the stock market, a Labor Act that would define the rights of workers as they had never been defined before, and a revival of antitrust regulations to *prevent* businesses from forming organizations for cooperation—just the opposite of the policy under NRA. There was an about-face in policy, to be sure; but there was no change in Franklin's major purpose: to get the economy going again and to free its citizens from want.

(18)

WHEN the "honeymoon" period is over, most Presidents begin to find that they may have been too optimistic in saying what they will do if they are elected. There is a good deal of difference between looking at problems as a campaigner and actually having to solve them as President.

Of course, the public memory is short and political promises are often forgotten; but this is much less true of those promises that affect people's welfare or the national security. About such issues the President is expected to achieve what he has promised.

But the Congress, he finds, does not feel that it has been bound. Not even the party platform necessarily binds Congressmen. Parties stretch over a wide range of views and their members may represent many differing interests. Except for election purposes, party pronouncements are honored or not as the individual Congressman decides.

Franklin found the Congress cooperative so long as there was a crisis. He had no trouble getting appropriations for relief and for bolstering the banking system. But when it came to the program he gradually worked out for recovery and reform, the opposition organized itself very quickly. His honeymoon, like those of other Presidents, was soon over.

One of Uncle Ted's most telling symbolic epithets for the conservatives who had opposed him had been "malefactors of great wealth." The corresponding symbol for this later Roosevelt's feeling about them was "economic royalists"—a phrase he used with enormous effect in his campaign for re-election in 1936.

Most of the "economic royalists" were Republicans; but not all of them were. And most of the liberals were Democrats; but not all of them were. Franklin had been nominated and elected as a Democrat, but he made it understood that he was at least as much liberal as Democrat, and he made no party distinctions in the support he accepted.

Different proposals thus got different receptions from the Congress. In the beginning, there were even some that were accepted more enthusiastically than Franklin liked.

The most important of these centered about his desire to raise prices. Early in 1934, Franklin was seeking some way to restore the price level to about where it had been when most people had contracted debts. He tried to proceed cautiously, but there was one section of Franklin's party that wanted prices raised by any means and without limit, and who were determined to succeed. They felt that if enough money was in circulation, dollars would become so cheap that debtors could get enough of them to pay off their debts. This would stimulate the economy, and, because it would favor the debtors rather than the creditors, would help the small businessmen and farmers to get going again.

Creditors, of course, were against this, but for the most part they were conservative, Republican, and in the minority, and so could offer little effective opposition. But Franklin, too, was opposed to having the government simply put more money into circulation, for he was afraid of too radical a change in the value of the dollar.

It was an embarrassment to Franklin that members of his own party advocated inflation—the issuing of currency to relieve debtors (and lower the value of the individual dollar by so doing). And his embarrassment was made doubly acute by the fact that these same men opposed the NRA and AAA, feeling that such devices would not be needed if the President would follow their advice. The nice thing about inflation, they felt, was its automatic nature. The government would only need to print money and enforce competition. The complex job of bringing together and working out plans and agreements among many cooperating producers would therefore not be necessary.

The inflationists and the progressives were not always the same people; but they agreed in opposing the devices of the early New Deal and they were delighted when the NRA and AAA were declared unconstitutional.

Franklin, as we have seen, was disillusioned by the fact that businessmen had taken advantage of the NRA codes to fix prices and divide up markets, and he was unhappy to be displeasing the progressives. His remarkable turnabout was accompanied by a similar turnabout in his attitude toward the inflationists. He began to accept "reflation"—restoring the price level—knowing that by keeping up his spending program for relief and his public works programs, and by lifting prices, his progressive friends would close in behind him.

He determined to try buying and selling gold, as he was urged to do, to see whether the price level could be controlled in this way.

He had been thinking about this for some time, and conferring with a small group of economists about the actual operations involved. Henry Morgenthau, Jr., who had been in his New York State cabinet, was now Secretary of the Treasury. Morgenthau had been much influenced by Professors Warren and Pearson of Cornell where he himself had graduated. Actually they were professors in the College of Agriculture and not monetary experts, but they had conceived the management of gold prices to be a way of giving farmers relief from their burden of debt. (With higher prices—eventually stable prices—farmers' debts could be paid more easily; and normal activities would then be resumed.)

It was this scheme that Franklin resorted to in some desperation when relief, easy credit, public works, and the Blue Eagle campaign failed to stimulate industrial activity and banish unemployment.

The government, the only buyer of gold, would fix its prices, and from day to day gradually increase it, thus increasing the value of each ounce of gold and, of course, decreasing that of each dollar.

The scheme, when tried, turned out to be only partially successful because, as Franklin learned, gold was less important in exchange than the Cornell professors had thought. Most transactions were now made by check and the relation of bank credits to gold was not direct. Prices rose somewhat, but activity did not resume; and presently Franklin asked the Congress for a law fixing the dollar at 56.9 per cent of its former gold value. He thus gave up the scheme of manipulating price level by daily purchases.

One measure passed during the Congressional session of 1935 overshadows in retrospect every other achievement of the New Deal. This was the passage of the Social Security Act. To trace its development we must understand conditions in the winter of 1934–35. At that time, the economy continued to lag, and unemployment remained high. Farmers were now being paid for controlling production, but they were grumbling about the increase in prices of the goods they had to buy. Consumers, too, were annoyed because the processing tax made food cost more.

During that session of the Congress, added appropriations for relief and public works had to be requested. These had at first been granted because of the obvious need. Most of the responsibility for putting the appropriations to good use now would fall on the relief organization, since Hopkins had at least shown how people could be put to work rapidly. A Civil Works Administration was set up; he was made administrator; and jobs were created by the thousands all over the country.

But when spring came in 1934 and Franklin had been President for a year, things were not much better. The immediate stress had been relieved by the emergency relief measures; but these had no permanence. He decided, when the Congress got ready to adjourn, to announce that he would be ready with a social security plan when the next session assembled.

This was a shrewd move. People were worn out not only with actual hardships but with the uncertainties of bad times.

Many had stood daily in bread lines, or had had to meet the rent or make payments on their homes with the help of relief money. Many businessmen had faced or gone through bankruptcy. Young people had had to give up dreams of education.

People were longing for an end to emergency measures. A system of security, set up permanently on the solid base of joint contributions by workers and employers, to ease old-age hazards; and a system of contributions to a fund that would take care of other risks—disabilities, widowhood, unemployment—these would be a wonderful change from the hazards and hardships of daily life.

There was some opposition. The idea that the federal government had any responsibility at all for the welfare of individual citizens was still very strange to many people. They saw it as an opening wedge to "socialism" and the end of the free enterprise system. There was, in fact, a furor about this first social security proposal that is difficult to understand by those old enough to have seen its benefits but not old enough to recall the fight for its adoption.

Belief in "free enterprise" was something close to a religion for the American people. They identified it with the pioneer spirit and traditional virtues. "Rugged individualism" was held responsible for developing the nation into a world power in less than half a century. So, in spite of the miseries arising out of the failures of the free enterprise system to prevent depressions, the belief still persisted that every individual could make his own way in the world and if he failed, it was his own fault.

However, although this individualistic attitude was widespread, those who had some knowledge of what went on in other countries knew that social insurance was successful in Britain, in Germany, and elsewhere. It had in fact been adopted many years before and no nation where it existed would think of giving it up.

The Democratic National Platform of 1932 had advocated "unemployment and old-age insurance under State laws." So when Franklin appointed a committee to recommend "safeguards against misfortunes which cannot be wholly eliminated in this man-made world of ours" he was redeeming a pledge, even if only a vague one.

Actually he was acting from deep conviction. He had had experience as Governor with the tragedy of unemployment, and the despair and humiliation of worthy citizens who had been caught and crushed in the national misfortune through no fault of their own. And he had learned how inadequate state treasuries were to alleviate such miseries in times of stress. He was determined that it would never happen again.

It is a curious comment on the times that although the party platform advocated social insurance, there was actually not much support for establishing it. There is no doubt that if Franklin had not undertaken the leadership, and presented a plan, the pledge would have been forgotten. Even those who had suffered most from the results of the depression could not see why the federal government should take responsibility directly for welfare. To be sure, many states and municipalities had passed laws to provide for orphaned children and destitute old people, but not all by any means. And the assistance available under these laws was very meager; and when the Depression had persisted for some time the ability of states to carry the increased load of needy people quite disappeared.

Relief had had to be accepted; but no one liked it. It made no difference to people who had clung to rugged individualism generation after generation that the Depression had been caused by events beyond their control. They may have understood it intellectually but emotionally they still felt responsible, and they felt that government should not really become involved in providing security for illness or old age.

Because all the sources of public communication were hostile by 1935, very little of what Franklin proposed to do was allowed to come through to the public. The result was that his social security proposal was pictured as more "government interference." The fact that what he was proposing was essentially an insurance system was lost in the talk about "socialism" and "communism" as the Security Act was discussed.

Curiously enough, even the labor unions were at first opposed, because it seemed to compete with them. Their pension systems were relied on to induce workers to join, and leaders were afraid that if the benefits were extended even to nonunionists it would reduce their membership. Large farmers were opposed to it because they saw in it a lessening of their power over farm workers. Small farmers were not interested in it because, not being "workers," they would not receive its benefits. Businessmen and industrialists were naturally opposed to it because they would have to contribute to the pension of each of their workers.

It was only because Franklin used all the political prestige he had that the Congress consented to passing the law he suggested. Nevertheless it was finally done; and no achievement of his administration was more generally approved in later years.

(19)

FRANKLIN was able to get the social security bill passed because of his personal hold on the voters. In turn, the the gratitude of those who benefited increased that hold.

Presidents are elected every four years; but members of the House of Representatives have only two-year terms. Representatives thus run when the President does, but also every four years when he does not.

It is almost axiomatic that the opposition party makes gains in the odd years. For some reason, voters seem to express whatever disappointments they might have in a President by voting against his party in these off years.

It is almost a rule, too, that any President can be *renominated* for a second term; but *re-election* is another matter. (Hoover, for instance, was renominated, but lost the election because he was blamed for the unexpected depression.) Presidents in office have a big bureaucracy to work for them and are able to get much publicity. But if events have been unkind to them, they have to defend their record, and no matter how favorable that publicity, they still may lose.

The 1934 Congressional election broke the rule. The Democrats gained House seats instead of losing them. This seemed to be a decisive endorsement of the New Deal, and Franklin felt that he himself had such support that he could go on as he had been doing.

The election of 1936 supported this belief. He was nominated for a second term without opposition and was re-elected by a bigger margin than in 1932.

He may not have brought about complete recovery; but

he had gone a long way toward establishing economic equality among Americans, and in giving them a renewed sense of being valuable individuals. Workers no longer had to carry all the risks of the free enterprise system. Their right to bargain and their claim on the wealth of the nation when in trouble had been guaranteed.

A later generation, looking back at the events of the Roosevelt Administration, may be puzzled to observe that these impressive endorsements came to the party and the candidate in spite of continuous criticism in the press, a criticism which rose at election time to an almost hysterical intensity. The secret, of course, lay in the confidence people felt in Franklin's intentions. Also, what his critics offered seemed to them much like what they had had before—and did not like. All the talk about danger to the Republic if Franklin was continued in office fell on deaf ears. The conservatives were even foolish enough to oppose spending for relief, and, in 1936, mounted a campaign against social security. This made it plain to the voters who were their friends and who were their enemies. It is quite possible that the intemperate opposition was an advantage since it made Franklin's position and that of his opponents so clear.

But the endorsement that came to him was won with more than deeds. Franklin never neglected to point out the gains and excuse the losses. When the press was most heavily weighted with criticism, he could say that it was the principle of equality that was under attack. His enemies, he said, wanted power again, so that they could have their old privileges. In press conferences, he answered questions freely, hostile as well as friendly ones, and, in spite of their reluctance, the newspapers could not refuse to print much of what he said. He often spoke over the radio, and millions of families listened in their homes. He developed a way of addressing them—simply yet comprehensively—that carried them along with him.

He traveled a good deal. This, too, annoyed his opponents because the appearances he made throughout the country were so effective. Crowds came to see and hear him and individuals felt themselves rewarded if they were one of thousands to whom he spoke.

One of his advantages was his amazingly detailed knowledge of all phases of national life. This, and his obvious urge to improve everything, gave whatever he said an intimate interest. He wanted towns to have better streets, hospitals, schools, post offices, water and sewer systems, parks and playgrounds. Many such facilities were actually being built. Almost every community had some project, needed for a long time, that now was being undertaken. The supplemental activities of the Civil Works Administration (which in 1935 became the Works Progress Administration [WPA], with a renewed appropriation) had become more efficient and more useful. In cities such as New York and Chicago—and smaller ones as well—the housekeeping jobs that had been neglected during the depression's early years were now being carried out at federal expense. The CCC was operating to everyone's satisfaction. Not only were the boys happy in their outdoor environment, but the parks and forests were demonstrating the effects of their work. The more permanent and costly projects of the Public Works Administration began to show great rewards. It was satisfying to know that the country was really being improved.

Eleanor also traveled a great deal, listening to people's troubles and asking questions. She took her reports back to Franklin and was often able to surprise his administrators with an intimate knowledge of their successes and failures. She had a priceless knack for projecting a precise picture of the conditions when she described them to her husband. And, of course, he talked with numerous other people of all sorts every day. The formal reports from his administrators were helpful; but sometimes he surprised them with more knowledge than they themselves possessed.

When the Congress passed the appropriation bill of 1935 it empowered him to allocate the funds among the various agencies. This allowed him to establish by Executive order the Works Progress Administration and the Resettlement Administration. This last was an attempt to bring to poorer folk in the farming areas more of the benefits that were going to those who lived in the cities, and it marked a significant step in his fight for national recovery.

It had been customary in the past to overlook the results of the long depression among the poorer farmers. It was assumed that they at least had a home and could grow food for themselves. But this assumption was not always true. Many did not own their homes or their gardens; and many others lived in villages without any more resources than city people had.

There were many more of these people in the 1930's than there would be later when the drift to the cities had become a tidal flow. There were, in fact, far more farm laborers and sharecroppers than there were independent farmers. Homelessness was a problem involving not a few but many millions of families.

The Resettlement Administration undertook to find farms for the dispossessed and better land for those whose land was so poor it would not yield a living. It had funds to loan for improving operations under the supervision of management experts. An important part of its program was to retire altogether from production much land that ought not to be cultivated but used instead for recreational areas, parks, and forests.

Resettlement became a favorite object of attack by the conservatives, particularly by the more prosperous farmers. They were benefiting from the Agricultural Adjustment Administration whereas the poorer country people were not. The larger farmers wanted to keep their poor dependents so that they would always have a supply of cheap labor.

Unfortunately, because the wealthy farmers and their associations influenced such a large number of Congressmen, and because Congressmen from nonagricultural states had little interest in the problem, it became increasingly difficult to get appropriations for many of the activities of the Resettlement Administration. Eventually it was so curtailed that much of the good it might have done was never accomplished. But this had not yet happened in 1936.

What may have been as important as anything in bringing about Franklin's remarkable election victory in 1936 was another disaster added to the vast one of the depression. The Depression defeated Hoover in 1932; the worst drought in memory helped to defeat Landon, Franklin's Republican opponent in 1936.

In 1934 and 1936 the prairies beyond the Mississippi simply dried up. There was little snow in the winters to feed the underground springs; and in summer the sun burned up the vegetation, leaving the land bare. Starving cattle and sheep ate the grasses down to the roots; and when the winds came the dust blew up in clouds until the air was thick. It drifted against the fences and left the subsoil exposed where crops had once grown.

These clouds of dust carried far toward the East. One day, when a Department of Agriculture expert was testifying before a Congressional committee, he interrupted his remarks, drew back the curtains, and pointed dramatically to the billows blowing in from the West.

Even when it did not blow away, the land was made useless for a long time to come. The droughts came to a country that never should have been broken to the plow. These droughts were known to afflict the short-grass plains regularly, in cycles. But the high price of wheat during the war had lured farmers farther and farther west into drier and drier country. It had been only a matter of time until the succession of favorable years would be broken and the droughts would come.

From a green beginning in the spring of 1934, the country beyond the Mississippi, and especially in western Kansas, Nebraska, and the Dakotas, had a complete crop failure in the months that followed. Then eastern Colorado, Oklahoma, and Texas began to show signs of blowing. The southern areas began to be called "the dust bowl."

Thousands of discouraged farmers whose land had blown

away began to load their few household possessions in jalopies, and, with the children fitted in wherever they could find space, rolled over the highways to California seeking a new chance.

These "Okies" and "Arkies" settled anywhere they could find shelter, often in tents along irrigation ditches and in eucalyptus groves. They had no money to make a new beginning; and there was very little work available in the orchards and groves. The owners of the ranches in California and the welfare authorities were soon so overwhelmed that the Resettlement Administration undertook to build a series of camps where these refugees could live. This helped, but it was not enough.

The year 1935 was somewhat more favorable for farmers. A crop was produced and the AAA compliance checks were going out. But then the winter of 1936 was as dry as that of 1934 had been. Crops were planted; but there was no snow to melt in spring and supply the moisture for growing. It did not rain. As April came, and then May, the blowing began again —and so did the parade of jalopies along the roads to the coast. The relief agencies tried to keep many families from joining the movement by making grants of money and providing work. At one time three-quarters of the families in the dust bowl were getting some sort of government help. But the migration was nevertheless a formidable movement.

It was more than a local disaster; it was a national problem. The President had diverted as much of his emergency funds as he could to relief in this area, and the struggle with nature was watched by the entire nation.

In the middle of the summer of 1936 after the party conventions had been held, Franklin went West to see for himself and to promise help. He had been renominated unanimously, of course, and the Republicans had chosen Alfred Landon, the Governor of Kansas, to run against him. To show the Administration's concern for the farmers' hardship, Franklin went first to Bismarck, North Dakota, and then traveled southward in a special train along little-used railway lines across the bare and burnt-out land. The train ran slowly and stopped often.

Franklin left it every day and went by automobile deeper into the stricken land, away from the railroad, talking with farmers and their wives, seeing businessmen in small towns, and, of course, conferring with political leaders.

He had insisted as he left Washington that it was a "nonpolitical" trip. But there was an election that fall and everything he did was bound to have political meaning. He had arranged a meeting in Des Moines with the Midwest governors. He would ask them, he said, whether everything possible was being done. Fresh from his explorations, he knew as well as they what conditions were. The meeting was not likely to produce any new ideas. However, one of its advantages was that Landon, his opponent, would have to come, since he was a governor; and he would have to acknowledge, even if not openly, that the Democratic Administration had saved thousands of families from starvation or migration.

The meeting was nonpolitical; but it was the most effective possible campaign maneuver. It dramatized the new policy of the federal government: People were its concern. And wherever they needed help its agents would go. They had gone to the drought country—and to the Pacific coast states—with generous help. Easterners, who might have felt that the West was sharing too much in the distribution of relief funds, were told through the many reporters who went with the President just how intense the need was.

As the President said, it was an illustration of the nation's oneness, of the concern of every part for every other part. He did not need to say that this concern was a Democratic and not a Republican policy.

There were other issues discussed during September and October in the campaign that followed; but none that came so close to people's hearts. Landon was a fine man and a good governor; but he was in a contest with the man Franklin's next opponent (Willkie, in 1940) would call "The Old Champ"; and he never had a chance.

Yet for all its eventual one-sidedness, the campaign of 1936 was filled with drama. The Republicans campaigned energetically, and they controlled the press (85 per cent of the newspapers declared themselves for Landon) and the radio. This made the outcome seem somewhat doubtful, and the professional politicians who, after all, organized party support, were anxious to de-emphasize those activities that were most criticized.

Resettlement and WPA bore the heaviest weight of the public attack. Resettlement, said the critics, helped only the shiftless, and work relief was no more than "boondoggling." This word became so dangerous that Franklin used the device of adopting it and asking whether it did not describe something necessary, rather than something ridiculous:

> There is a grand word going around—boondoggling. It is a pretty good word. If we can boondoggle our way out of the depression, that word is going to be enshrined in the hearts of the American people for years to come.

Papers, 1936, 58.

In one of his best campaign speeches, defending WPA, he asked whether it would really be better to have the workers strung out in bread lines, their families hungry and in fear of dispossession, rather than doing useful jobs—even if not very well. This work did allow men to take home pay checks which, when spent, helped support the economy.

It was a successful stroke. Grasping the nettle was, after all, better than apologizing and accommodating the conservative opposition.

However, Franklin made no attempt to defend the Resettlement program. The politicians felt that most of the poorer farmers did not vote, or at least could not make a serious contribution to the election. They listened to Congressmen from the farm states who in turn listened to the larger farmers opposed to Resettlement. That program, in fact, was marked for dissolution.

Opposition sprang up from another quarter. A right-wing organization called the Liberty League, made up of prominent and wealthy lawyers and businessmen, as well as such Demo-

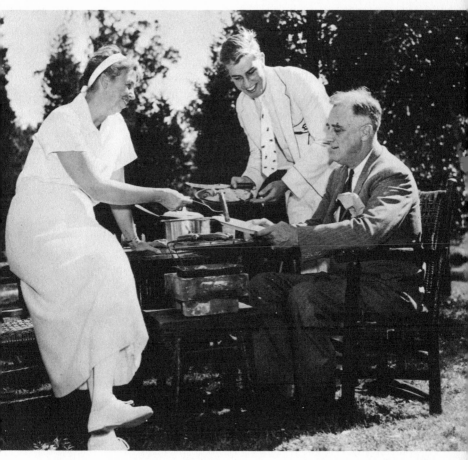

Picnicking with Eleanor and Franklin, Jr., at Hyde Park, 1935

crats as Al Smith and John W. Davis, former Democratic nominee for the Presidency, was loud in its denunciation of Roosevelt and his policies. Its members assured the nation that Franklin's re-election would destroy American institutions and pleaded with their listeners to vote for Landon.

But in the end neither the solemn warning of the Liberty League nor the more moderate arguments of Landon had much influence. Eight million more people than ever before voted in the election, and Roosevelt received the most overwhelming vote of approval ever accorded a Presidential candidate to that time. Of all the forty-eight states only Maine and Vermont went against him. The Republicans kept only the hard core of their membership in the Congress. It was, in truth, a landslide.

Now, Franklin felt, he was not merely President because Americans wanted to see the last of Hoover; he was approved for himself and his policies. He felt flowing to him that vast support a political leader cannot be sure of until the election returns are in. He would now go on to new accomplishments.

Or would he? He was too experienced a politician not to know that second-term Presidents often have trouble in controlling a legislature. Still, the 1936 election was a magnificent demonstration of popular support. It might suffice in a struggle with the Congress he could see coming.

(20)

WE spoke in the last chapter of Franklin's preoccupation with and success in meeting the farmers' problems. Before we go on to the discussion of his second administration, it would be well to consider the source of this interest.

On his frequent visits to Warm Springs from 1924 on, Franklin became almost as familiar with the countryside of Meriwether County, Georgia, as he had been with Dutchess County, New York. It was there, in fact, that he learned new lessons about farmers and their problems—and much of what he learned appalled him.

This was the old corn and cotton country. The cultivation of these crops for generations had caused erosion; and much of the topsoil had washed away into the streams. The fields were run down now, grown to brush and weeds almost as much as to crops.

This cause alone would have marked the people for poverty. But worn-out soil was not their only trouble. When Franklin became Governor, they were taking the full brunt of the post-war agricultural depression as well. Its marks were everywhere. And when he became President their situation was desperate. Old farm houses stood paintless and shabby in neglected yards; and year after year more land was abandoned. Cattle ran in scrubby fields and they were low-breed stock, not much good for either milk or meat.

New cotton lands had been opened in the West—in the Mississippi Delta, in Texas, in irrigated lands in Arizona and California. There the soil was richer, the crop more certain, and the cost of production lower.

Then too, the quantity of cotton, like the prairie crops of corn and wheat, had been enlarged enormously during the war; then, when the war was over, foreign markets were closed.

There was a surplus stored in warehouses that would fill the demand for years to come even if no more was produced. So naturally the price had fallen—and kept on falling. This was bad enough in the Mississippi Delta and in Texas; but in Georgia it was disastrous. Every farmer who grew cotton at all had much of it in storage. And since storage was costly and selling had to be at a loss, it was harder and harder to get the fertilizer and seed needed to grow another crop. As a result, it was difficult for these people to make enough money to buy food for their families.

To make the misery complete, the boll weevil had become a destructive pest, eating the heart out of developing plants. In time experts would bring it under control; but there were years when the fields that came up green and promising were eaten away before the crop could be gathered.

The country that surrounded Warm Springs suffered from all these ills. Franklin, who traveled about the countryside in a hand-operated car adapted especially for him, spent many an afternoon, in the years between 1924 and 1928, cruising along the country roads within easy driving distance of Warm Springs. He often stopped at farmers' houses, asked for a drink, perhaps, and sat talking with them in the shade of a chinaberry tree. His inquisitive mind gathered from what they had to say a full knowledge of the calamity they were struggling to survive.

Running over their situation again and again, he speculated on what might help. He could see that it was not enough for agricultural experiment stations to show how erosion could be stopped and the boll weevil eliminated. These were essential; but the trouble went deeper. Even if the productivity of those old fields could be restored—although even that seemed unlikely—there was the hard fact that too much cotton had reduced the price to five cents a pound (the wartime price of a few years before had been thirty, even forty cents). What could be done about that?

There were several possibilities he could think of. One was some measure that would raise prices to levels that would at least cover the costs of production. This would require the opening of a larger market than now existed. Could government restore foreign trade? Or could it find new uses for cotton? But above all, and even if demand could be enlarged, could some means be found to adjust production to consumers' demands?

These were not his responsibilities, at least not yet; but he could think about them. When he first came to West Georgia, he was something more than just a New Yorker visiting the Springs to see whether he could get back the use of his legs. He had been a public figure once even if he no longer was. Also, he was of special interest to the local residents because he had bought the shabby old resort property and was turning it into a rehabilitation center for polio victims. This was an exciting occurrence in that dull neighborhood, and the influx of activity would help the community. Still, no one guessed that he might one day be President and thus actually be able to do something about the distress of the corn and cotton country.

It was recalled that he had been the Democratic candidate for Vice-President a few years before; and it was noticed that whenever he came, the local political leaders gathered around, and even those from Atlanta and other southern centers came to call. If Franklin could do nothing—being out of public life altogether—about governmental action to help the farmers (the restoration of foreign markets or a national program of crop control), he might make some contribution in another way.

He considered this, and discussed it with his friend Cason Calloway, who was a textile mill operator. Calloway had for a long time been using some of his profits to improve his enormous estates. What he had accomplished was in itself a demonstration of the kind that always fascinated Franklin. On the

Calloway farms there were herds of purebred cattle running in carefully kept pastures; and there were other crops as substitutes for cotton.

This interest in agriculture was a bond between these two extraordinary men, so different yet so much alike. Both had the impulse to create, to shape things around them, to manage men and to improve whatever they looked at. Franklin was often at the Calloway home, even after he became President. Turnley Walker has described such visits:

> He sometimes spent an evening with his old friend Cason Calloway at Blue Springs. Here Graham Jackson, a Negro musician from Atlanta, would come to play and sing for him. . . . Jackson was an old friend by this time, having been brought to the White House in Washington in the earliest Presidential days by an Atlanta politico. . . . After the group singing was over, Roosevelt would motion Jackson to his chair and take his arm in the easy way he had with everyone.
>
> "Play me a little quiet music, Graham."
>
> And Graham would sit on the arm of the chair and make his loud-voiced instrument go very soft. Sometimes he sat on the floor and, as he played, rested one arm on the big man's knee where he could feel the hard rounded prongs of the braces, and, looking up, he could see the heavy head come down, relaxed, and the weary eyelids closing.

> Turnley Walker, *Roosevelt and the Warm Springs Story,* New York, 1953, 236.

When the Depression struck industry the Calloway mills were as hard-hit as others. During Franklin's visits to Warm Springs from 1929 to 1932 (when he was Governor of New York) he found the distress in the small towns as bad as that on the farms. Calloway tried to help his workers. He was paternal with his labor, built them homes and churches and community facilities; but he was against unions and violently unwilling to negotiate with them about anything.

He saw, however, that the problem of the Depression was larger than could be solved by any one employer; it was something that affected the whole economy. Some of the conversations between him and Franklin were curious. Calloway hung on to his conservatism; Franklin was more and more convinced that drastic action would be necessary, governmental action to rescue farmers and to start industry going again. Neither was given to philosophical conversation. Both preferred to think and talk about what could be done. And they were most at one when they discussed the rehabilitation of the old cotton country. Calloway was demonstrating certain new possibilities on his land. Franklin decided to join this effort in his own way—by buying a farm with poor prospects on Pine Mountain, Georgia, and seeing whether he could show others that it could be made productive.

The farm he chose was not an extensive operation like Calloway's, whose holdings ran to thousands of acres. Such estates might be suitable for experimenting with new crops and livestock; but they are not very helpful in showing the ordinary farmer what he could do. On his Pine Mountain place Franklin set out to see if he could demonstrate something of practical use to his neighbors.

Since he did not intend to create a gentleman's estate, but wanted to see whether he could demonstrate new methods his neighbors could use, he tried everything that was suggested by the farmers around him.

As cotton had failed, many farmers had begun to raise cattle. But because both their resources and their knowledge were limited, the herds were scraggly and the beef they produced was tough and stringy. Better-bred herds, more carefully tended and fed, might change this. It was one of the experiments Franklin tried.

He also thought that instead of letting their old fields go to brush and weeds, many farmers could plant long-leaf pine trees—one called the "loblolly" seemed especially promising for producing lumber and pulpwood. In addition, at the suggestion of Calloway, who drew on his own experience, he tried peaches, apples, and grapes.

Calloway did all he could to make Franklin's farm a success; he even furnished much of the planting stock; but the enterprise never prospered. This was partly because the land was too elevated and dry and the soil too eroded. But it was also because Franklin visited Pine Mountain less frequently after he became absorbed again into public life, and he had to depend on hired managers. They were faithful but they had very little to work with. Only heavy investment and the most careful management could have made the farm a success. Altogether the venture was a failure.

Calloway's large farms were productive exceptions to the general bankruptcy of West Georgia farming. They did show that much could be done with the old cotton lands. But the owner was always there to manage things; and the situation of his land was in favorable valleys, not on high ridges.

The significance of this agricultural venture in the Roosevelt story is not what was done on Pine Mountain, but what he learned from it that was of use afterward. He failed to produce a paying alternative for cotton and corn; but this was not because none could have been found, but rather because without much capital and good management the hard conditions would defeat the small farmers. They needed sources of credit, they needed education, they needed more careful advice. And even then, perhaps, the enterprise would need to be on a scale they could not reach.

When it is suggested that certain New Deal ideas came into Franklin's mind at Warm Springs, what is meant is that his sympathy for a poverty-stricken people, together with his failure as a private demonstrator to help them, taught him how necessary it was that they should have assistance. What he had missed knowing about when he was a boy, he had learned about as a man.

Thus when Franklin became President, his determination to improve the farmers' situation showed itself in many ways. At first, it must be acknowledged, his new agencies were of little use to those who were worst off—those on worn-out land or tenants and sharecroppers without any land at all. But farmers on better land, who suffered from the Depression

The author, FDR, and Secret Service man leaving the site
for Greenbelt, Maryland, 1936

more than from permanent handicaps, were helped by the easier credit facilities and from the adjustment programs devised in Franklin's first Presidential years. They made a relatively quick comeback and were soon prospering again.

For the others—and there were millions of them—who were much like the people he got to know so well in southwest Georgia, something more was needed. This is what the Resettlement Administration was meant to supply, and when the hostility of Representatives from the agricultural regions showed itself in reduced appropriations—ones that eventually disappeared altogether—Franklin was gravely disappointed. Resettlement failed, but the failure was not of his making.

In contrast with this, the Civilian Conservation Corps and the Tennessee Valley Authority were continued and enlarged. The TVA operated in only one region, of course, and Franklin's hope that it might be the first of several river valley improvement authorities was not realized. The CCC went on to do useful conservation work until 1943, when young men were needed to fight rather than to improve forests and parks.

In sum, West Georgia's farm people got less help from the New Deal than Franklin had hoped. But they did share in emergency expenditures, and whatever additional federal help Franklin could give them, he did. Erosion was checked and the price of cotton rose; the boll weevil was ultimately checked. One of the WPA community projects was set up nearby and continued for some time until its small homesteads ceased to be a community and merely became homes for workers who commuted to factories in the towns.

As for Pine Mountain itself, most of it was made into a state park. Of the many visitors who now come to visit Franklin's southern home, most want to see the Little White House and many ask about the polio center. Only a few know about or inquire about the farm. If they do ask and find out where it used to be, they are only able to see the top of a ridge, partly reforested, partly grown up to brush and weeds. There is nothing more.

(2 1)

AS Franklin's second term as President began, there were new issues to face. The challenge to democracy from the totalitarians was coming closer and closer. Hitler was now the master of Germany and was obviously preparing to conquer all Europe.

Recovery was not yet complete in the United States; but there had been gains. The social security system was getting started; and in time it would take the place of many relief agencies intended only for the emergency. The country could then settle down to making progress in the traditional American way. That is, it could if it was allowed to. But Franklin could already foresee that there might have to be a mighty mobilization of the whole democratic world. Italy and its pretentious Fascism was not a world threat. The National Socialism of Germany was far more formidable.

Germany was not only a big nation, but it had shown again and again the power of disciplined effort. The Atlantic Ocean between Europe and America was no longer the absolute protection it once had been. The airplane was fast developing and might become within a few years an offensive weapon with intercontinental reach.

The threat was not immediate; but it was not really so far off that it could be ignored. It was a President's duty, as Franklin saw it, to tell the people what confronted them. They must be aroused to prepare for resistance. In his annual message in 1935, he had warned of trouble in Europe:

> I cannot with candor tell you that international relationships are improved . . . old jealousies are resurrected, old passions

aroused; new strivings for armaments and power, in more than one land, rear their ugly heads. I hope that calm counsel and constructive leadership will provide the steadying influence and the time necessary for the coming of new and more practical forms of government throughout the world wherein power and privilege will occupy a lesser place and world welfare a greater. . . .

Papers, 1935, 24.

He knew the response would be reluctant. Disillusion about the results of the last war still lingered. There were many who would resist strongly any suggestion of interfering again in any European quarrel. It was Franklin's job to convince them that their own security was involved.

It seemed to most Americans then that the Nazis lived in a world of fantasy. Hitler's talk about "Nordic supremacy" and his claim that other races were inferior simply seemed nonsense. And when he said that the democracies were decadent and would be swept away before the wave of the future represented by Nazism, most people simply yawned or laughed. But Franklin was well aware that the threat was far more serious than it seemed because it had the great power of Germany behind it.

In Italy Mussolini had made himself dictator before Hitler had become Chancellor of the Reich in Germany. The Italians called themselves "Fascists," but their ideas were much like those of the Nazis, that is to say "totalitarian." They believed in dictatorship of an "elite," and, of course, Mussolini and his associates were the elite.

The Germans probably did not regard the Italians as very useful military allies, but Franklin foresaw that when the Nazis' aggressiveness really broke out into attempts at conquest, the two nations would inevitably stand together in an attempt to subdue all Europe—and then look for further conquests.

It would be hard to convince Americans that all this could be dangerous to them. It was usual to think of Europe as a remote place and of its people as rather like characters in a story. What they did or what they planned did not really matter.

The First World War should have proved to Americans how mistaken this was. But when President Wilson had tried to turn the Allied victory into a permanent peace, he was quickly shown that interest in the Allies' future had evaporated.

Franklin, campaigning in 1920, had found that even those Americans who had been soldiers believed the United States should stay out of European quarrels. This had been a severe lesson to him; and in the campaign of 1932, after considering the issue, he had let it alone. This still held true in 1936. The foreign relations of the first Roosevelt term were confined mostly to working out agreements with other nations to trade more freely.

What concerned the voters was the cost of living (always going up); what should be done about labor conditions; the demands of farmers; taxes; tariffs; monetary policy—bread and butter matters.

Leaving foreign affairs alone may have been good politics; but it was very bad policy. Continuing to assume that nothing happening across the sea could possibly matter encouraged foreign leaders to think that they could behave as they liked without interference by the United States.

The Germans had mistakenly relied on this in 1917. It was obvious that Hitler and his advisers were relying on it again. They were oppressing the Jews, restricting religious practices, clamoring more and more loudly about their need for *Lebensraum* and building a powerful military force. Franklin often discussed these sinister signs with his advisers; and he made it as plain as he could to the public in interviews and speeches that Hitler must be checked.

Nevertheless, it was not a campaign issue. If elections were to be won, they must be won on the issues people were interested in; and, following professional advice not to discuss unpopular topics, Franklin avoided foreign affairs. In 1936, the issue was the record of the Administration over the past four years.

During the year or two following the great victory of 1936, domestic issues would continue to be more pressing. There would be a struggle with the Supreme Court in 1937; and this would involve the need for establishing by law at least some of the fair practices the industrial codes had been intended to maintain. The NRA had been simply abandoned when the Court said it was unconstitutional; but it was different when the AAA was disapproved. Something had to be devised that would make the farmers' situation more secure and that would not be rejected by the Court.

This was found in a "conservation" bill providing for compensation to farmers who would turn away from wheat or cotton—of which vast surpluses existed—and grow soil-building crops—legumes and grasses, mostly, or trees. This would also result, the Department of Agriculture pointed out, in an increase of the protein foods—milk and meat—so badly needed by those with low incomes.

Problems of this sort, that had to be attended to at once, made it seem possible to neglect the issue of most significance for the future—the showdown about to take place between the democratic and totalitarian powers. Britain and France would actually challenge Hitler in 1939; but in 1938 the preliminary moves were already being made. Franklin was deeply concerned as he watched. But few Americans were interested.

It was not only the indifference of people in the United States that encouraged the totalitarians to think their fantastic and brutal behavior would not cause any interference from outside. The British were in an appeasing mood. Their statesmen were making only mild objections—so mild, in fact, that Hitler grew bolder and bolder in his aggressions. He finally absorbed Austria, took over the Sudeten part of Czechoslovakia, and made preparations to march further eastward. In the end he went too far. When he invaded Poland in 1939 the British and French had either to honor their treaty of mutual assistance with that nation or expect Hitler to turn on them when his appetite could no longer be satisfied in Eastern Europe.

Franklin watched these developments with growing worry. It was his belief that Hitler was incorrigible, a madman who would not be stopped by rebukes or even by threats. He saw, and soon began to say, that democracy could not co-exist with totalitarianism. One or the other must prevail. It was of the essence of Nazism that it must always go further. It existed for conquest. What had gained Hitler his German leadership was his inflation of the national ego after the humiliations of defeat in war and the long sacrifices needed to pay the excessive reparations demanded by the victors.

In 1936 he had sent troops into the Rhineland, still occupied by France, and waited to see what would happen. When there was no reaction except talk, his aggressions grew bolder and more confident.

Hitler believed himself infallible; and since each of his successive moves succeeded, he came to believe that he was destined to rule the world. The German people were willing to accept the discipline necessary to establishing themselves as the master race he said they were.

But the British and French had their sticking point. Even though they fully understood the power of the German military force and knew themselves to be much weaker, they felt compelled to check him. As for the United States, Hitler did not think the possibility of its interference worth considering at all. Roosevelt might disapprove of him and his policies, but what could he do? There was not only a determined isolationism for such a politician to deal with (enough to keep the United States uninvolved no matter what happened to Eastern Europe), but there were many Americans who thought National Socialism a superior form of government.

It is strange now to consider how the cult of totalitarianism spread in the United States during the depression years. What Hitler offered the Germans was security. If the German people would surrender their freedom and live as he dictated he would

With Congressman Lyndon B. Johnson at Galveston, Texas, 1937

take care of them. And because Franklin did not find a way to end the depression, only ways to relieve it temporarily, many Americans—especially the well-to-do—wondered aloud whether the order and discipline of Germany and Italy were not preferable to the awkwardness and inefficiencies, the arguments and internal struggles, of democracy.

Some very prominent people held these views. And they had a certain ready-made following in the large German population. Even if these immigrants were good Americans, they had suffered along with everyone else from the Depression. They saw that Hitler, by undertaking huge building projects and enlarging the military forces, was eliminating unemployment altogether, something even the astronomical expenditures of Roosevelt seemed unable to accomplish.

These people also felt a certain pride in the transformation of Germany from a beaten and occupied nation into a proud and powerful one. They overlooked, or did not believe, the stories of atrocities and oppressions. These, they felt, were either outright lies or were exaggerated; they were probably propaganda. They could see only that Germany was rising again.

The weakness of many American leaders for the Nazi-Fascist doctrine and the admiration of Hitler among descendants of German immigrants, made Franklin's problem a serious one. He never for a moment proposed to compromise with the alien doctrine. But he could see ahead of him a tedious and wearing effort. He felt it his duty to teach America that Hitlerism and democracy could not live together on the same planet. He had to use every means to strengthen and support those in Britain and France who saw the future crisis as he did and would have to meet its first shocks.

At the same time he was sensitive to the rise of a similar philosophy in Japan across the other ocean. It too was aggressive. Its dictatorial militarists were seizing more and more power on the Asia mainland. Sooner or later like would move toward like. It was a real possibility that a pincers movement might succeed, Japan moving westward, Germany eastward, and the two meeting in Egypt. They would then divide the world.

It seemed that way to Franklin; but in 1936–37 such a forecast seemed utterly fantastic to most others. What he could do to awaken his countrymen to the danger, he did; but they continued to be apathetic when he spoke of what he was more and more certain was coming.

(22)

THE over-all picture of Franklin's second term presents a contrast between his own awareness of danger from abroad and the American people's desire for additional reforms and economic improvement at home.

As time went on, the American public began to accept his views, and no political campaign after 1936 was without a debate on foreign affairs. At first, very few Americans were willing to consider active intervention, but a growing number would learn from the events of the next years that passive isolationism was the worst danger of all.

But when Franklin was inaugurated for his second term in January, 1937, he was forced to concentrate on domestic problems. These were, after all, the problems that during the campaign he had pledged he would devote himself to after his election.

There *were* still troubles at home. The depression continued to loom large in everyone's thoughts. Most people were far from satisfied that everything that could be done had been done—and they were right.

One reason for this was uncertainty over objectives: should the government strive for an over-all reform of the entire American economic system, or should it simply do everything it could in a limited way to make sure the economic system recovered but did not radically change? Then there was Franklin's inability to get Congress to do what he wanted —we shall see how important this was as we go on. There was even division over economic policy—very deep division. The Brandeis-Frankfurter-Corcoran group—whose influence Franklin had accepted when he saw that the results of his

FDR, 1937

early experiment in business-government cooperation (NRA) was failing—was determined that big business should be cut down to small competing units. This implied more effort by the regulatory agencies such as the Federal Trade Commission and the creation of such new ones as the Securities and Exchange Commission (1935) to police the stock market. Also it meant putting new life into the Anti-Trust Division of the Department of Justice to prosecute monopolists, and this further infuriated the businessmen, who disapproved strongly of all governmental interference.

But disclosures following the panic phase of the depression had shown widespread use by bankers of their depositors' funds for speculation. When the market collapsed, losses had been immense. Senator Black, later to be a Supreme Court Justice, and Ferdinand Pecora, acting as counsel for a Senate investigating committee, uncovered intolerable abuses. Even the oldest and most prestigious financiers, including J. P. Morgan, the grand panjandrum of Wall Street, were unmercifully grilled, and an incredible indifference to ordinary rules of honesty were disclosed. All bankers were touched with discredit, and some previously thought to be eminently respectable were prosecuted and sent to jail.

Set against this corruption was the behavior of Franklin himself as President. His concern for the general public welfare furnished an example of democratic responsibility, as did the openness and informality of his manner. Franklin knew very well how important it was to maintain the democratic style, and sometimes spoke of it:

Yesterday, at Hyde Park, a distinguished European writer, a great biographer, was visiting me; and yesterday afternoon over back of our place, at what we call "the cottage," we had a little picnic. We had some neighbors there, and we had some members of the press. And this great biographer was perfectly amazed because there we were, sitting around in our shirt sleeves, some going swimming in the pool, and everybody having a good time. He said: "You know, if this happened anywhere in Europe, whether it was a Dictatorship, or a Monarchy,

or a Republic, the head of the nation would have been surrounded by men in uniform, soldiers with bayonets, and the
members of the press would have appeared in frock coats and
silk hats instead of shirt sleeves and bathing suits." . . . I am
very confident of the future of this country as long as we maintain the democracy of our manner and the democracy of our
hearts.

Papers, 1935.

Franklin's conception of the President as teacher led him
to keep in close touch with the public. While the severe measures were being prepared for regulating the speculators who
had been exposed during the investigation, he carefully kept
the public informed.

He took special care to explain what was being done. Com-
mercial (or deposit) banking was being separated from investment banking so that depositors' funds could not be used
by the bankers for speculation, and a reserve to insure against
the kind of losses that had followed the bank closings of the
depression years was being devised. All this he explained with
great care.

These measures, together with the Securities and Exchange
Commission and changes in the Federal Reserve system to
strengthen governmental supervision of banking, completed
the program of banking reform.

These changes were not made without furious objection
by the bankers. Their protests were bitter, and because the
press was now completely hostile to the Administration, they
were given the widest possible hearing. However, these protests, which started before and continued through and after
the 1936 election, were helpful rather than harmful to the
reformers. The louder the bankers complained, the more certain the American public was that the Administration was
working in their interest.

From his first entry into politics, Franklin had followed
the progressive line. He had begun with his fight against
Sheehan's election to the United States Senate by the New

York State Legislature, and he had continued with his early commitment to Wilson and his own campaign for the Vice-Presidency.

Even though Cox had lost in 1920, Franklin was certain that the choice between progressivism and conservatism, as exemplified by this election, would be a continuing choice for the American voter, and he was equally convinced that progressivism would have its day. He had thus continued to follow the progressive tradition even while out of office.

In this he had been right. The violence of the swing surprised even him; but he and his party had been in a perfect position to profit from it in 1932. And now, in 1937, when the Democrats were at the crest of their power, the progressive program, never finished by Wilsonians because the war had intervened, could be advanced. The banking reforms represented part of this advance.

Meanwhile, we have seen that some of the early acts of the New Deal—the NRA, the AAA, and the various credit institutions—went beyond the older progressive tradition. The Brains Trust had felt that these were a necessary change of method to get the same result: the protection of the public interest. They had felt, moreover, that their methods would result in recovery but that the older reform measures would not. There could be no real well-being, they argued, unless production could be increased. There must be more to share as well as equality in sharing. They hoped for a joint governmental-industrial collaboration, with government always the senior partner but not a repressive one.

The orthodox progressives were not interested so much in increased productivity as in reform. And, as we have seen, after two years they had their way. But there was no recovery —or very little. Unemployment was still at a dangerously high level; productivity did not increase very much; and people's distresses continued to be relieved primarily through various transitory relief measures—by this time, public works mostly. The Social Security Act had been passed (progressives and collectivists agreed on the desirability of this) but it would require some years to be useful. So the economic situation showed very little actual improvement. The Brains Trust felt that their program would have produced better results, but by that time they were outsiders with no influence. Franklin, after his brief leaning toward collectivism, was firmly back in Brandeis' progressive camp where he had started.

He could feel that in pushing reform measures he was acting in the tradition of Bryan, Wilson, and other predecessor progressives; also, that he had the full support of Brandeis, to whom he had looked for approval most of his life. Not only this, but the complaints of the bankers and business leaders were wonderfully effective political arguments in his favor. The Depression was still alive in voters' minds; disclosures had convinced them that it had been caused largely by misbehavior in the business world; the Administration was rooting out the evil they had suffered from. They would not vote the party of business back into power.

All this was part of Franklin's justification for the abandonment of collectivism and adoption of government regulation of business. In 1936 he was back in the White House with a renewed mandate, and he could now virtually ignore his detractors. Two years after his inauguration, in a 1939 message to Congress, he spoke of the resolution of the conflict between progressivism and collectivism:

> We have now passed the period of internal conflict in the launching of our program of social reform. Our full energies may now be released to invigorate the processes of recovery in order to preserve our reforms.

Papers, 1939, 7.

(**23**)

AS a politician, Franklin was enormously pleased by the victory of 1936. It seemed to ratify all that he had done and to suggest that the voters would like more of the same. If he was overconfident—that was the excuse. Perhaps he ought not to have read into the results more than was warranted; but the fact is that he did. He undertook, on the strength of his showing, to subdue the Supreme Court, as he put it, to the will of the people; and in the fight that followed the Congress, always jealous of Presidential power, saw its chance to defeat him and took it.

The quarrel between the President and the Supreme Court had been boiling up for some time. When, in May, 1935, the Court struck down the NRA as unconstitutional, it had said:

> Section 3 of the Recovery Act is without precedent. It supplies no standards for any trade, industry, or activity. It does not prescribe rules of conduct. Instead . . . authorizes the making of codes to prescribe them. . . . In view of the scope of that broad declaration, and of the nature of the few restrictions that are imposed, the discretion of the President in approving or prescribing codes, and thus enacting laws for the government of trade and industry throughout the country is virtually unfettered. We think the code-making authority thus conferred is an unconstitutional delegation of legislative power.

Papers, 1935, 221.

Franklin did not choose to strike back too hard in 1935, but his anger was nevertheless evident:

> You see the implications of the decision. . . . It is one of the most important ever rendered. . . . And the issue is not going

162

to be a partisan issue for one minute. The issue is to be whether we go one way or the other. Don't call it right or left; it is a question for national decision on a very important problem of government. We are the only nation in the world that has not solved the problem. We thought we were solving it, and now it has been thrown right straight in our faces. We have been relegated to the horse-and-buggy definition of interstate commerce.

Franklin went no further than this kind of statement then. He was waiting for the election results before he made a more definite move.

True, he was quite ready to make changes in some of the agencies the Court had invalidated; but he would rather have reformed their operations from within than to have been told by the Court that it must be done. Now he felt strong enough to show the Justices that they could not successfully oppose needed reforms. He spoke out against the Court at the beginning of 1937:

> The Democratic Administration and the Congress made a gallant, sincere effort to raise wages, to reduce hours, to abolish child labor, to eliminate unfair trade practices.
>
> We tried to establish machinery to adjust the relations between employer and employee.
>
> And what happened?
>
> You know who assumed the power to veto, and did veto, that program.
>
> The Railroad Retirement Act, the National Recovery Act and the Guffey Coal Act were successively outlawed. . . .
>
> Soon thereafter the nation was told by a judicial pronunciamento that although the Federal government had thus been rendered powerless to touch the problem of hours and wages, the States were equally helpless; and that it pleased the "personal economic predilections" of a majority of the Court that we live in a nation where there is no legal power anywhere to deal with its most difficult, practical problems—a No Man's Land of final futility.

Papers, 1937, 118.

Antagonism among the three branches of our government was intended by the authors of the Constitution; President, Congress, and the Supreme Court are often in disagreement. Franklin was not the first President to feel restrictions imposed by the Justices, nor, indeed, the first to be annoyed by them. But what Franklin either did not recognize or chose to ignore was that the Court by now has accumulated an enormous prestige. Its opinions, especially among the more conservative, were next to sacred. There was, as Judge Jerome Frank once said, "a cult of the robe."

There is, of course, nothing in the Constitution that authorizes the Court to declare acts of the Congress to be unconstitutional. All the branches were made independent as well as interdependent. It follows that Presidents may take their own view of what is and what is not permissible. But in a series of decisions famous in history, Chief Justice Marshall and his successors had assumed the power of interpretation and had not been challenged in exercising it.

That doctrine of judicial supremacy had been accepted so long that most people actually thought it was part of the Constitution; and most of those who knew better still regarded it as desirable. There had, however, been considerable stretches of time in American history when the Court had taken upon itself the duty to overthrow any legislation that threatened to limit property rights, regulate business, or promote welfare. One of the more serious of these, afterward reversed, was the rejection of a federal income tax. In these instances, the measures rejected had almost always been sponsored by Presidents; and they were usually resentful. Sometimes, like Franklin, they fought back.

There was one weakness in the Court's position. This was the constitutional provision that its composition and jurisdiction were to be fixed by the Congress. And, of course, its budgets had to be provided from the same source. It was this that gave Franklin his opening. He knew that the number of Justices had been changed in the past when the Court had opposed generally desired reforms. And he now proposed something similar.

While the election victory was still fresh in people's minds he and Attorney General Cummings drafted a reorganization act; and just after the Congressional session began in 1937 he asked the Congress to pass it. It provided for an added number of Justices whenever a member of the Court reached the age of seventy and did not retire. This would give him an opportunity to appoint his own men, and this is how he proposed it to Congress:

> If we increase the personnel of the Courts so that cases may be promptly decided in the first instance, and may be given prompt hearing on appeals; if we invigorate the Courts by the infusion of new blood; if we grant the Court further power in maintaining the efficiency of the Federal judiciary; and if we assure government participation in the speedier consideration of all constitutional questions, we shall go a long way toward our high objectives. If these measures achieve their aim, we may be relieved of the necessity of considering fundamental changes in the powers of the Courts. . . .

Papers, 1937, 59.

There were a number of other provisions intended to modernize administration of all the federal courts; but it was this point that was at once seized on by opponents as an attempt to bend the judicial process to the Presidential will.

His critics were able to ridicule the argument put forward in his accompanying message that men over seventy had lost their ability to sympathize with progressive measures, and that they were anchored to the past, and that their views were bound to be reactionary. Since the most liberal of the Justices at that time—such as Brandeis and Cardozo—were those who were past seventy, this did not seem a valid argument even to Franklin's supporters. It left him open to the charge—made loudly and at once—that he was only seeking an excuse to get his own way without judicial interference.

The proposal for Court reform ("packing," his opponents called it) did not seem important at first; but it became immensely swollen very rapidly, and the resulting struggle grew to be one of the most dramatic of his whole Presidency. Many of those he must have counted on in the Congress to support him turned against him; and before long he found himself the object of a bitter and sometimes vicious attack. It was he who was on the defensive, it seemed, rather than the Court. Here is Franklin speaking at a Democratic victory dinner in March, 1937:

> I defy anyone to read the opinions in the TVA case and the AAA case and tell us exactly what we can do as a national government. . . .
> The language of the decisions . . . creates doubts and difficulties for almost everything we have promised to fight for—help for the crippled, for the blind, for the mothers—insurance for the unemployed—security for the aged—protection of the consumer against monopoly and speculation—protection of the investor—the wiping out of slums—cheaper electricity for the homes and on the farms of America. You and I owe it to ourselves, individually, as a party, and as a nation to remove these doubts and difficulties.

Papers, 1937, 119.

He lost. His bill was not even passed in amended form. It was simply voted down, and this by a Senate that was overwhelmingly Democratic. It could be seen afterward that there were a number of immediate reasons for this. His envoys were inept in persuading Senators; and he could no longer offer patronage as he had at the beginning of his first term. Also he lost his majority leader at the climax of the fight: Senator Joseph Robinson died suddenly of a heart attack. But the basic reason for defeat was that he ran head on into a century of accumulating Supreme Court prestige. He was therefore asking the Congress to do something it would do only under tremendous public pressure; and even his usually loyal public seemed to be against him on this issue. He had not succeeded in making it understood.

He was amazed. He had expected so easy a victory that he had not taken the trouble to prepare as he would have done for a real conflict. On other issues he had shown immense resourcefulness in getting his own way. He had carefully canvassed Congressional opinion in advance, and where it was necessary, he had persuaded enough potential dissenters to come over to his side. When the issue was important enough, he had "gone to the people." Many Presidents before him had followed this course. And since Presidents can command so much attention their arguments are always heard. Often reluctant Congressmen are forced by their constituents to support Presidential proposals even when they do not like them. If they hear from home in volume they are persuaded.

Franklin thought his campaign arguments had brought him the necessary public support. He thought too that a reactionary Supreme Court would be recognized as a potential danger by all those who were benefiting from the New Deal. Labor's rights, the farmers' ability to control their own operations—both curtailed by the decisions of the past year—would, he thought, bring him allies. He was mistaken. The Court had become too sacred.

The Court protected itself too by unexpectedly approving several New Deal laws while the issue was being discussed. Also, Justice Van Devanter, one of the most reactionary, resigned, and was replaced by the liberal Hugo Black. These moves were generally attributed to the clever management of Chief Justice Hughes, who, without appearing in the open, directed the defensive strategy.

It could be seen afterward that practically all Franklin's suggestions for modernization were necessary. In fact all of them, except the provision for enlarging the number of Justices, were later adopted. Much later, Franklin was able to say this:

Whatever doubts were created by the old Court before the

elections of 1936, have been removed. There has been a re-affirmation of the ancient principle that the power to legislate resides in the Congress and not in the Court; and that the Court has no right to impose its own ideas of legislative policy, or its own social and economic views, upon the law of the land.

The result has been that the federal government now has the undisputed powers which had always been intended for it by the framers of the constitution.

Papers, 1937, *Introduction.* [This summary was made by the President several years after his struggle with the Court.]

But Franklin's humiliation was at the time complete.

This Court incident was in itself less important than the indication it gave of what was to come. The Congress had been annoyed during the last several years by the taunt that it was merely a "rubber stamp" for the President. It was in a dangerous mood. And the election results had not modified the feeling very much; in fact there was a disposition to show Franklin that the Congress was still an independent body in spite of the President's popularity.

Here we see one of the familiar characteristics of our government. The Congress by nature opposes the President when it can. Its independence is precious to its members; and legislative leaders have proclaimed at many tense moments that it is for the Congress to make policy and for the President only to execute it.

The months of economic crisis, when the Congress had so gladly accepted Presidential leadership, were over. Political realists reminded each other that custom denied Presidents more than two terms. And Franklin, therefore, was thought to be nearing retirement. His hold on the electorate would be loosened; and Congressmen need no longer fear his "going to the people." They could safely assert themselves.

The importance of this change of mood was to become more and more serious as time went on. The United States would soon need to make historic choices of immense consequence. In another two years war would begin in Europe;

decisions would have to be made about supporting one side or the other; and dissension would come close to tearing the country apart. Never would there be more need for a strong President than in the time just ahead—and strong leadership is virtually impossible with little or no Congressional support.

Franklin's humiliation in the Supreme Court fight was more, then, than just a setback. It was evidence that during the rest of his second term he could not count on Congressional co-operation. Their Supreme Court victory elated the conservative Congressmen. They now felt they could liquidate most of the New Deal and prevent any further "experiments."

(**24**)

THE worst worry of Franklin's first term had been the stubborn sluggishness of the economy. Year after year, unemployment refused to disappear; and relief and work relief had to be paid for. Reforms, as the Brains Trust had argued, tended rather to hinder than to encourage, recovery. There was always a budgetary deficit; the Congress could appropriate new funds but this did not bring income to the Treasury.

When more is paid out than is taken in, governments simply print money to pay for the difference, and, when the number of dollars is increased in relation to the goods and services to be bought (food, shelter, doctor bills, and so on), prices rise. However, when goods and services cost more without an accompanying increase in wages, consumers begin to resist. They buy less.

Franklin had hoped to raise prices by buying and selling gold, but one of the difficulties was exactly that when prices did rise, customers could buy less. Franklin's idea that the clearing away of debts would allow activity to start again was all very well. But when they had been cleared away, and when people who had been debtors were ready to begin buying again, they found that prices had risen so high that even if they wanted to pay what was asked, they could not buy as much as they wanted. And so demand was checked. This was a dilemma; and there was trouble for Franklin in the slowness of improvement. In 1937 there was another crisis—a sinking spell that recalled the terrible times of a few years before. Its immediate cause was Franklin's attempt, just after election, to reduce expenditures for relief and public works. He seems to have confused the good feeling after the election with actual recovery. At any rate he felt it was time to reduce spending. The reiterated charges during the campaign that the Administration was "lavish with public funds" had annoyed him. But he was now to learn what he seems not to have fully realized before (although he had said that he did): when consumers cannot buy, the economy will not prosper. This leads to the economic conclusion that the balancing of national budgets is not done by reducing expenditures, but by increasing production and wages. When activity is intense and incomes are high, the taxes on them yield more. At the same time a rising level absorbs the unemployed so that they can support themselves and can make larger contributions to production.

This was not the old-fashioned economics that Franklin had learned at Harvard; but it was the theory that best suited the complex modern economy. If this had not been demonstrated before, it was made clear by the renewed depression of 1937.

In the middle of that winter, the economic situation became so serious that Franklin had to cancel his economy moves and ask the Congress for renewed emergency funds. Relief measures of all sorts were enlarged again and gradually matters improved. Members of the Brains Trust, now all out of government, felt that their views had been justified.

When he spoke to the Congress at the beginning of 1938 he seemed to have learned a lesson. He said:

Again I revert to the increase of national purchasing power as the underlying necessity of the day. If you increase that purchasing power for the farmers and for . . . those in both groups who have the least of it today, you will increase the purchasing power of the final third of our population—those who transport and distribute the products of farm and factory, and those of the professions who serve all groups. I have tried to make clear to you, and through you, to the people of the United States, that this is an urgency which must be met by complete and not by partial action. . . .

I am as anxious as any banker or industrialist or businessman or investor or economist that the budget of the United

States be brought into balance as quickly as possible. But I lay down certain conditions. . . .

. . . That we continue the policy of not permitting any needy American who can and is willing to work to starve because the Federal government does not provide the work.

That the Congress and the Executive join hands in eliminating any Federal activity which can be eliminated without harming necessary government functions or the safety of the nation.

That we raise the purchasing power of the nation to the point that the taxes on this purchasing power—or in other words, the Nation's income—will be sufficient to meet the necessary expenditures of government.

Papers, 1938, 7.

But these were not easy conditions, and no one expected them to be met very soon. Almost at once Franklin was to ask for extraordinary appropriations for defense as well as for unemployment relief. This foreshadowed something that would solve one problem even if it brought many others. Unemployment would disappear in swelling activity as defense expenditures increased; but the budget would never be balanced while Franklin was President.

The fact is that he never did find the way out of his dilemma. Deficits continued to pile up, and the national debt grew larger year after year. Apparently this did not worry the voters too much; but it worried Franklin. His reforms were now in operation; and the outrage of businessmen was being muted as they saw that what had been done could after all be lived with. Their chastisement in the 1936 election had taught them to be more cautious; but they were still not willing to undertake the vast ventures supposed to be characteristic of Americans; and only such an enlargement of enterprise would bring the national product up to the level it ought long ago to have reached.

It was the beginning of war in Europe, and the tremendous effort required to supply the Allies with munitions, together with American expenditures for defense, that finally furnished the solution. Spending for these purposes was more than

Franklin had dared propose for recovery purposes even after the lesson of 1937. Government expenditures increased tremendously month by month after 1938, and it was instructive to see unemployment diminish month after month as production increased under the stimulus. Welfare expenditures could then be reduced month by month too; and the levels of

FDR, his mother, and Eleanor with George VI and his wife,
Queen Elizabeth, Hyde Park, 1939

ASSOCIATED PRESS

living could go up and up. It was learned, to everyone's amazement, that the expense of huge war preparations—both for the United States and for the Allies—could be met, and yet that people could have more income to spend than they had ever had before. The change in the circumstances of workers was startling. That the budget was badly unbalanced seemed nothing to worry about.

The lesson was clear. The levels of productivity must be high and must continue to rise. Whatever methods were necessary for bringing this about must be accepted; the increase was its own justification.

It became easy, first with defense and later with the war as the reasons, to go easy on big business and to keep only those reforms that defined and enforced fairness in labor relations. This, in fact, is what happened as the country shifted its concern from domestic problems to foreign ones.

Americans soon had to make up their minds whether they would support one or the other of the warring groups in Europe (and there *was* much support for the German-Italian axis). Then, once this decision was made, they had the far more difficult decision of how deeply involved in the European war they would become.

The nagging problems of the past years, budgetary deficits, business complaints, the worry over paying for relief and public works—all faded out as the nation got ready for war, or for "defense" as Franklin felt compelled to call it. When it began to be understood that the United States would one way or another be involved in Europe, nothing else was of much comparative importance.

Vast appropriations were now voted without any of the reluctance that much smaller ones for relief of various kinds had aroused. The nation slid without recognition from one era into another. In the new one, governmental responsibility for welfare would never be questioned again. Balanced budgets would never again seem more important than food and shelter for citizens. It would be understood that high productivity must be the aim of economic policy.

(25)

AFTER Franklin's difficulties with the Congress in 1936 and 1937, the Congressional elections of 1938 had a particular importance. Would the legislators who had been so quick to repudiate Presidential leadership and to refuse him the laws he wanted, be re-elected? If they were, they would be more independent then ever. But if the worst of Franklin's enemies could be punished by defeat, this would give him renewed influence in getting what he wanted.

His difficulty was not wholly that of disputing with the Congress; this was in a way expected, although he had hoped to soften it. There was also the fact that he was now going into the latter half of his second term, and this was presumed to be his last. Presently ambitious politicians who hoped to be his successor would appear; and during 1939 and 1940 the party professionals would be maneuvering to pick the candidate they preferred. It was assumed that little attention would be paid to his wishes either about a successor or about matters that ought to be attended to if the country were not to stand still.

And it ought not to stand still. There were decisions to be made, and much to be done. Emergence from the Depression was not at all complete. The sinking spell in 1937 had shown dramatically that the economic spiral had not yet turned decisively upward. There were also the totalitarians in Europe, becoming more aggressive and threatening. The country had to be alerted. Altogether it was important that Franklin's position with the public be confirmed and that he should gather the support he needed to keep things going.

Since he himself would not be running for office in 1938,

this would not be easy. It could only be done by breaking an old political rule, carefully observed by most Presidents before Franklin, against interfering in off-year elections. He made up his mind that he must try, supporting some candidates and asking for the defeat of others. True, it had often been shown that local workers reacted against such interference, and for good reason. Members of the Congress were elected to represent their districts or their states. They were judged by their practical services—by the bacon they brought home—rather than by their performance as national statesmen. If the President said to people in Georgia, for instance, that their Senator had behaved badly in national matters, the Georgia Senator had only to respond that he had been industrious in getting the federal government to favor Georgia with jobs and projects.

This kind of argument actually was made. Walter George was the senior Senator from Georgia. His long service had made him almost a tradition. He had been re-elected many times; and his home organization had grown powerful with patronage.

But he was an extreme conservative, and had opposed Franklin more often than he had supported him. He had been especially determined in the Supreme Court fight. Franklin thought that here he had a chance of demonstrating his ability to reward or punish. He asked the people of Georgia to defeat the Senator who had so often opposed him:

Let me make it clear that he is, and I hope always will be, my personal friend. But there are other gentlemen in the Senate and in the House for whom I have an affectionate regard, but with whom I differ heartily and sincerely on the principles and policies of how the Government of the United States ought to be run.

The test lies . . . in the answer to two questions: First, has the record of the candidate shown, while differing perhaps in details, a constant active fighting attitude in favor of the broad objectives of the party and of the government as they are constituted today; and, secondly, does the candidate, really, in the heart, deep down in his heart, believe in those objectives? I regret that in the case of my friend Senator George, I cannot honestly answer either of these questions in the affirmative.

Papers, 1938, 469.

He thought of this struggle, also, as testing his long political cultivation of the South. Since 1924 he had been speaking of Meriwether County as his "second home." He had frequently consulted southern leaders and often addressed Georgia audiences. Would they follow him or would they hold to their long-time support of the Senator?

Having determined to break the rule of Presidential neutrality, the only thing to do was to make the tests those that he might have a chance of winning. Thus he interfered only in those instances—like that of Senator George—where he felt himself strong. But he calculated that if he prevailed in these tests he would have a manageable majority in the next Congress. Then he could go on with his program.

He was not completely successful in his attempts. In the case of Senator George, the failure was conspicuous because it was there that he felt he had his best chance. In fact, his Georgia defeat was so much talked about that the instances in which the voters took his advice were generally overlooked. But they amounted to half the contests. There was a conspicuous victory for Franklin in New York where Congressman O'Connor was badly defeated on the issue of opposition to the President.

In the end, Franklin did not get the Congressional majority he wanted; but his successes did show him and influential politicians that he had immense backing among the voters.

Even if he did not wholly succeed he felt that the effort had been worthwhile. The hostility of the Congress had become too serious to be ignored or accepted. When it is recalled that 1938 was the year when the Allies abased themselves before the Nazis at Munich, when Mussolini was completing his brutal conquest of Ethiopia, when the Japanese were settling themselves in the heart of China, and when the legitimate Spanish government was being overthrown by Franco's rebels

—supported by Italian and German forces—it can be understood how necessary it was that the nation should have a leader who could build up the nation's strength.

The partial failure of what the hostile press called "the purge" did not, however, close one other way to check the decline of his influence. He might let it get around that he would stay in office—that he would be a candidate for a third term. If, instead of retiring after 1940, he seemed likely to go on in the White House, his wishes might be much more respected. Repeated surveys showed that quarrels with the Congress had in no way affected his popularity. He knew that in spite of these quarrels, he could have the nomination if he wanted it. His political backing was too strong to be overcome in the convention.

Getting nominated, of course, is very different from getting elected. National nominating conventions are meetings of politicians from all over the country who control local organizations. The delegates from the states and districts always outnumber members of the Congress from Washington. And these two groups are likely to support different candidates. In fact, local leaders are quite often suspicious that Washington people are only interested in being re-elected themselves. This suspicion was strong in 1939–40. The people back home were Roosevelt supporters, and members of the Congress were well aware that, if Franklin asked for the nomination, they could not defeat him.

Franklin's support, in other words, had by now changed radically. It was not the leaders who had nominated him in 1932 and who now wanted to keep him in office. It was a new crowd. They were, in fact, those who had been against him before. The city bosses in New York, Chicago, and other cities had been for Smith in 1932. However, their machines had thrived on federal relief and they were now among Franklin's most ardent supporters. They were reinforced by labor leaders who had so vastly enlarged their membership under the New Deal.

Franklin no longer belonged to the old Democratic Party

178

—that of Farley, Garner, and the southerners. He belonged to a new one, one that owed its existence to the welfare measures he had sponsored. The Congressional conservatives might have in mind a man of their own to succeed him in 1940—in fact, they did—but if Franklin asked for the nomination his new backers would certainly be able to get it for him. In fact, they were likely to urge it on him whether he asked for it or not.

The conservatives had only one weapon to stop him: the strong prejudice against any President running for a third term. The tradition of *not* running had been respected since George Washington had established it at the end of his second term. Opponents began very early to use this argument. From what was said it might have been thought that there was such a prohibition in the Constitution; and no doubt there were many who felt that if it was not there it ought to be.

What Franklin's own position in respect to a third term was during 1939 and the early part of 1940 is difficult to say. He often spoke of his longing for retirement, but the ordeals he was having with Congress and the formidable European situation stiffened his resolve to see the country through its crisis. He did not say in the winter or spring of 1940 that he would run again; but he also did not say that he would not. When his supporters began to suggest it, he merely turned aside questions about it as premature. But he also made no attempt to throw his support behind other possible Presidential candidates—men who might have thought as he did and might carry on the programs he had started.

Franklin's consent was delayed until the very last moment. But from the time when a third term was first suggested, strength began to gather behind the demand for his candidacy. By the summer of 1940 it was satisfactorily convincing.

The political argument was, of course, overshadowed by the threat of war, but it was strong enough to cause some defections from the Democratic Party. For instance, James A. Farley resigned. He had been Postmaster General and Chairman of the Democratic Party, and had worked hard in

Campaigning in Newburgh, N.Y., 1940

the first two campaigns. But he was offended now, he said, by the breaking of the third-term tradition. Actually, he felt his hold on the party so strong that he could use it to get the nomination for himself. Then there was Vice-President Garner, who had come to office with Franklin in 1932 but who now opposed him openly. So it went. The Party simply split on this issue. (One of the interesting results of the

180

divisions of 1940 was that Harry Hopkins, who had moved from one job to another after starting as Relief Administrator, emerged as a politician. He represented Franklin at the convention, substituting for the disaffected Farley.

The convention was held in Chicago in the early summer. As the time approached, Franklin had not yet committed himself to a third term. What would happen, he asked himself, if he retired? More specifically, what would happen to his New Deal programs if a conservative, even one from his own party, was elected?

There were indications that this might happen. Those most often mentioned as his successors among the Democrats belonged to the conservative wing—Secretary Hull and Farley himself among them. They would have Vice-President Garner's support—and they had had enough of Franklin and his New Deal.

They wanted to go back to the older fiscal policies. The budget would be balanced, and most of the new welfare agencies—the Public Works Administration, the CCC, the Home Loan Corporation, the Agricultural program, and so on—would be abandoned. They were too costly. Taxes would be reduced, and unemployment would be ignored. If families were in want, local government or private charities could look after them as they had in the past.

At convention time, however, it was quite clear the Democratic voters wanted Franklin and no one else. And it was this that reduced to despair those who would have replaced him if they could. There was such a demand that Franklin had only to consent; he did not have to ask. Since a third term would be unconventional, he thought it best to be drafted. And this is what he allowed to develop. Harold Gosnell, in his book *Champion Campaigner,* described the maneuvering at the convention most vividly:

Harry Hopkins, with a private wire to the White House in the bathroom of his suite in the Blackstone Hotel, was the President's self-appointed manager. This was a most unusual situation for a man who was not even a delegate. Ed Flynn was at Hopkins' side to soften the blow, and they passed the word along that Roosevelt would run again if drafted. Many of the party regulars were jealous of Hopkins' power, and they resented the way in which the convention was run. . . .

To add bitterness to the cup the delegates were forced to drink, word came from the White House that the "Boss's" choice for Vice-President was Henry Wallace, Secretary of Agriculture. This was too much for some of the delegates and their followers in the galleries. There were rumblings and catcalls.

Frances Perkins telephoned the President to come to the convention and calm the delegates. FDR would not move. He did not have to run. If they didn't like Wallace, then he, FDR, would bow out. He added that the Missus might go to the convention.

Eleanor Roosevelt did go to the convention, and she did a masterful job. She lifted the sights of the hot and tired delegates. The world was on fire. The man in the White House was doing his best to protect the country. It was no time for petty political squabbles.

Eleanor's speech turned the tide.

Gosnell, *Champion Campaigner,* 175.

Thus the city bosses, the labor leaders, and the western progressives carried the nomination for Franklin while he stayed in the White House and seemed to pay little attention to what was going on. The old guard of the party accused him of hanging on to the Presidency for sinister reasons. He prized the power it gave him, they said; he intended using the office to establish socialism or even communism.

Franklin made little effort to refute them. He could stay aloof from politics and still win. And, in fact, much of the political activity even before the convention was carried on by Eleanor, who traveled the country lecturing and maintaining contacts between the government and its people. She was invaluable to Franklin during this period, and if he did not seek her advice on major policy matters, she was nevertheless a definite liberal force in his Administration. Her moral indignation over the plight of the American poor and the atrocities of the European totalitarians, expressed in a daily newspaper column, periodic radio programs, and lectures, made her a national figure in her own right and identified the Roosevelt Administration even more strongly with the moral principles in which most Americans believed. As an example of her almost evangelical power, here is an excerpt from a speech on unemployment and the resources of the young at a youth meeting, as reported in *Time* on March 6, 1939:

Now, I believe in the Social Security Act. I believe in old-age pensions. I think we have to deal that way with many things. I believe in the National Youth Administration, not as a fundamental answer, but simply as something which gives hope, which gives perhaps a suggestion which might be followed by communities; never because the Federal Government could answer the whole problem of the unemployment of youth by a Youth Administration or WPA. It can't be done. These are stop-gaps. We bought ourselves time to think. That is what we have done.

There is no use kidding ourselves. We have got to face it together. . . . It is not just Youth. To be sure it matters more to Youth. Youth wants to begin living, it is vital for them. But we have all got to face it and face it together. . . . This goes down to the roots of whether civilization goes on or whether civilization dies. . . . It is nothing new for a civilization to come to an end. We have seen it happen over and over again. It is just a question of whether we have the brains to keep it from happening and the determination and the character and the unselfishness. It is a great challenge to the people of this country because we are the leading country today. We have bought ourselves time. Is it going to be worth buying?

Franklin's nomination, never really in question, was a strong rebuff to the conservatives, and the Farley-Garner group was left out in the cold. Once more, Franklin had unquestionably captured the Democratic Party.

(26)

IN the two years preceding the election of 1940 Franklin's troubles with the Congress were continuous, and almost no legislation of importance was passed. In the 1938 Congressional elections the Republicans had gained eighty-two seats in the House and eight in the Senate. Franklin's attempt to get a loyal majority had failed. The Republicans and the southern conservatives, between them, were able to maintain the coalition that had begun to form as soon as there had been some recovery from the panic of 1929–33. They were able to dominate the Congress.

But there were two policies Franklin felt to be essential for the nation's future and he must do his best, in spite of opposition, to see them carried out. If he could not get Congressional action, he felt, he could at least educate the public and eventually he would prevail.

One policy was perfecting and making secure the New Deal's advances in welfare—the social security system, collective bargaining in industry, farm relief, the regulation of financial institutions, the Tennessee Valley Authority, and the Civilian Conservation Corps. The other was support for the democracies across the Atlantic in the war Hitler seemed determined to provoke. This was a policy that must be accepted, if not at once, at least in time to prevent disaster.

A peculiarity of the struggle he had to carry on was that the progressive Democrats were determined isolationists, and that the conservative Democrats, who favored involvement in Europe, were enemies of the New Deal. With the party so divided how could he hope to make progress in either field?

The idea of collective security—the name given to the

184

policy of cooperation with Britain and France against the totalitarians—was regarded by Franklin's old progressive friends in both parties as certain to risk unnecessary dangers. They felt that it would lead to more and more involvement in European affairs—not much different from the intervention in 1917 that had taken the nation into a fruitless war. Most of these progressives came from the West—La Follette, for instance, from Wisconsin, Johnson from California, and Wheeler from Montana. They were strongly opposed to collective security. And as Franklin began openly to oppose Hitler and Mussolini, and to favor supporting France and Britain, they became more and more resentful.

Franklin, however, was certain that support of the Allies was necessary to the safety of the republic. Better, he thought, to have the fighting go on in Europe with American support than to risk the defeat of Britain and France and leave the United States open to attack.

A *Time* article of March 13, 1939, described the conflict between the President and the isolationist Senators:

In 14 minutes, without making a single amendment, the House last week passed a $499,857,936 supply bill for the War Department, including $50,000,000 for 565 of the planes called for in Franklin Roosevelt's emergency rearmament program.

Mr. Roosevelt's policy toward Europe was now definitely known to place the defensive frontier of democracy in France. Toward Asia, Mr. Roosevelt wanted to extend the U.S. defensive frontier to Guam, but the House had stopped him at Wake Island. Senators who disapprove of Mr. Roosevelt's frontier extensions fell huffing and puffing upon his air corps expansions as unjustifiable.

Idaho's ursine Borah, still weak from flu, denounced the air bill as dictated by "bluff and jitterism." His new junior colleague, pretty David Worth Clark, 36, made a maiden speech telling the U.S. to mind its own business. Minnesota's heavy Lundeen talked darkly of Presidential secrets which would "stun" and "shock" the country if revealed. California's white-crowned Hiram Johnson, North Dakota's "Neutrality" Nye, Missouri's chubby Bennett Clark all raised their voices in favor of what Massachusetts' prosy Walsh called national "detachment."

More embarrassing than Senate orations to Franklin Roosevelt was a proposal of twelve Senators with Wisconsin's cherubic La Follette as their spokesman, who introduced a modification of 1937's defeated war-referendum amendment to the Constitution which would effectively shackle the Administration with diplomatic handcuffs.

A year ago the Administration managed by only 21 votes in the House to beat the proposal by Indiana's Louis Ludlow that the Constitution be altered to require, except in case the U.S. was invaded, a national referendum before Congress could declare war on a foreign power. As revised by the twelve Senators, the proposed amendment would take from Congress the power to declare war except in case of "attack by armed forces, actual or immediately threatened" upon U.S. territory or upon "any country in the Western Hemisphere" threatened by a non-American nation.

Said Spokesman La Follette: "Americans have not forgotten the steps that made a declaration of war inevitable in 1917. War breaks out in foreign lands. The Executive decides to help one side. The nation becomes involved in secret commitments and breaches of neutrality. Then there are 'episodes' and excuses for taking sides further. . . . When it is too late to be neutral, Congress is asked to rubber stamp a declaration of war, and the people are lured by fancy slogans about fighting to end all war and save democracy. After the supreme sacrifice is made, democracy is destroyed and the peace settlement lays the groundwork for the next war."

With a last puff the Senate passed the air bill, amended it to up total planes—5,500 to 6,000.

Thus collective security became the issue Franklin felt to be of first importance. He was supported in this by the conservatives who had been against him in all his other policies— Senator George of Georgia and the other southerners, for example. Because it was so important, and because he had to have their support, he had to compromise on the projects they did not like.

For this reason much of the New Deal was traded away for their support. The two measures he insisted on were, first, the building up of American military forces, and second, aid for the Allies so that when they were intolerably pressed they would be able to oppose Hitler. The purpose behind this was to make such a show of strength that the totalitarians would realize that further aggression would only lead to their defeat.

It was obvious, however, that this was not enough. In 1938, in a conference at Munich, Hitler had won from the European allies an agreement that they would not interfere with his aggression in Eastern Europe. The concessions, as the British Prime Minister Neville Chamberlain explained them, were an attempt to ensure "peace in our time," but they only encouraged Hitler to believe that the Allies were weak, and from that time on he pushed his expansionist plans with even greater ferocity. The word "Munich" always afterward would remind people that appeasement only puts off the inevitable reckoning with aggressors.

In 1939, the Germans invaded Poland. Hitler thought he could get away with this not only because of the British and French weakness at Munich and afterward, but because he had been able to make a deal with the Russians to divide with them the territory he was about to conquer.

German military strategists had always feared a two-front war. Hitler, in fact, had tried to persuade Britain to join him in attacking Russia. Failing that, and being determined to expand his empire—he said that the Reich needed *Lebensraum,* and that the Germans were a superior race and destined to rule the world—he made the cynical alliance with the Soviet Union which, after Poland had been divided, would allow him to turn on Western Europe confident that his Eastern borders would be safe.

Franklin watched the development of Hitler's scheme with increasing anxiety.

He made speech after speech as the aggressors won battle

after battle, and he did, to some extent, change the country's attitude, but still he was unable to convince the Congress or the public of the danger he saw so clearly.

By 1940 Franklin was tormented by previsions of what would come unless he could act. But it now began to seem to him a terrifying prospect whichever way Americans finally decided to go. If the present indifference remained unbroken and the Allies were defeated, he saw a world delivered to the savagery represented by Nazi purges, Italian massacres in Ethiopia, and Japanese atrocities in China. If finally there came an awakening, it was now so late that subjugation even of the United States was not impossible. He knew the power of German efficiency. He studied it closely, and the more closely, the more it alarmed him.

The Democratic Roosevelt, 489.

The year 1940 is often spoken of by historians as "the year of the undeclared war." The British and French were doing very little, and Franklin, who had to consider the election in November and temper his strategy somewhat to the tolerance of the isolationists and pro-Germans, was not able to speak out as fully as he wished. But still he made his warnings plain.

Twice in radio addresses he spoke of aiding the Allies; and in both he attacked those who would hold back.

In May, in a "fireside chat," he spoke of those who "were persuaded by minority groups that we could maintain our physical safety by retiring within our continental boundaries."

This was just after the full force of the German blitzkrieg technique—a sudden attack by all armed elements in overwhelming force—had been disclosed in Poland. And he said:

There are a few among us who have deliberately closed their eyes. . . . To those who did . . . the past two weeks have meant the shattering of many illusions . . . [and] with this rude awakening has come fear bordering on panic. I did not share those illusions. I do not share those fears. . . .

Papers, 1940, 231.

Then in June, when Mussolini invaded helpless southern France, he said:

> On this tenth day of June, 1940, the hand that held the dagger struck it into the back of its neighbor. . . . In our American unity we will extend to the opponents of force the material resources of this nation. . . .

Op. cit.

Nonetheless, right down to convention time in 1940 there was a strong sentiment in the country for keeping out of any more foreign wars.

(27)

BEYOND his responsibility to warn the people of the totalitarian menace, Franklin felt he had a responsibility to continue the program of social welfare he had started seven years before. It cannot be too often repeated that he was the first President to accept responsibility for the people's well-being. This meant that he must somehow see to it that those who wanted to work had jobs, or if there were not enough jobs, at least that they had unemployment benefits. Those who could not work because they were old or disabled must be provided for. And those families without a wage earner must be supported too.

The main efforts of this kind were two. One was to regulate the economic system so that it ran smoothly, provided plenty of jobs at fair pay and assured decent working conditions. The other was a system of insurance. Workers and employers would contribute to a fund; and when the workers were old or disabled they would have benefits they themselves had provided.

This the government must manage. The way had been opened, of course, by some of Franklin's predecessors. They had interfered to prevent or stop strikes, to regulate business (mostly to prevent unfair competition), and, in wartime (as in 1917–18), to make certain that enough food, ships, and guns were produced. But never before had there been a guarantee that everyone could have a job, or, having none that some support would be available to the dependent family.

In establishing this principle of governmental responsibility (it would not actually become a reality for many years) he continued to be opposed by those who did not agree. We have seen that those who opposed him had been strengthened in the

190

Congress by the election of 1938. Some of Franklin's reforms were by now untouchable by his political enemies; but there was much more to do, and for the two years before the 1940 elections, Franklin had been unable to do it.

The only way now was to win the election by an impressive margin. Franklin threw himself into the campaign with all his accustomed vigor. *Time* described the effort:

Old Campaigner: Once he had taken the field, Franklin Roosevelt went campaigning almost as if 1940 were any year, as if the race were any race. His train moved with the exact precision that years of organization and the power of the Presidency command. Every Democratic precinct chief knew exactly when the President would pass, knew just when to have his crowd assembled. First stop was Wilmington, Del., where four years ago the President tipped over the Republicans for the first time in 24 years. The train stopped. A huge station crowd roared expectantly. As always, the President let them wait a few minutes. At last the door opened; the crowd bellowed. Out came a grinning porter to polish the brass-work. Another minute, and the President made a carefully timed appearance, got off a little speech timed for the afternoon papers: a quotation of Lincoln's definition of liberty (in effect: liberty for the sheep is not liberty for the shepherd, nor for the wolf).

After a smooth endorsement of the stronger of two Delaware Democratic tickets, Shepherd Roosevelt left the sheep, went after the Republican wolf.

The trip around Philadelphia and Camden was a political masterpiece. Everywhere the itinerary avoided conservative or Republican districts; everywhere sought out factory areas, Democratic strongholds. Crowds were thick, enthusiastic.

He motored past City Hall, past signs, "Welcome Champ," Roosevelt For a 3rd, 4th, 5th Term," past thousands of faces that know Roosevelt and light up when he passes. "If there's any anti-third term sentiment in America, it isn't in the faces of the crowds," said Correspondent Alfred Stedman of the anti-Roosevelt St. Paul *Pioneer Press*.

"I love a Fight." That night the President took his case to the nation over the radio. Tickets to Convention Hall had been

carefully allotted to 14,500 of the faithful; actually 18,000 people jammed in; thousands more stood outside. When the President arrived on the stage at 9:12 P.M., the audience went mad as only good Democrats can, whistling, shouting, stamping.

Politically the speech was masterly. Thirty-two times the President accused his opposition (never mentioning Willkie by name) of deliberate falsification of fact. The burden of the address was prosperity: 1940's business figures contrasted with 1932's, 1929's.

Time, November 4, 1940.

The Republicans that year nominated a particularly able and eloquent adversary, Wendell L. Willkie, an Indiana lawyer who, as president of Commonwealth and Southern Company, a utilities holding corporation, had attracted widespread attention through a controversy with the TVA. Willkie was an attractive, energetic candidate whose views on foreign policy were much the same as Franklin's but whose domestic policies differed radically from the President's. Many of the conservative Democrat's supported him, and many others simply stayed quiescent—"took a walk," as Al Smith put it; and Smith was one of those who did.

The issue most discussed in the campaign, however, was not the New Deal. It was the war in Europe and whether Americans should take any part in it.

This came about because it was suddenly understood that some of the welfare measures were untouchable: even the Republicans did not attack social security any more. They preferred to have it forgotten that they had ever opposed it.

They still complained about extravagance, unbalanced budgets, and irresponsibility; they said that their administration would be more efficient. But they did not propose to go back to the old individualism.

Franklin, sensing this, made his appeal to those who were repelled and perhaps frightened by the revelation of German ruthlessness, and what might happen if Hitler went on unchecked.

It was remarked afterward that Franklin had seemed to be running more against Hitler than against Willkie; and there was some reason for saying it. At first he tried a tactic he had never used before—that of remaining above the battle and depending on others to campaign actively. That, and the solid popularity of his New Deal, he thought might be enough. But his reserve soon broke down and he began to campaign in the old familiar way, somewhat late, but actively. Here he is attacking the Republicans, and especially three Congressmen, Martin, Barton, and Fish:

> What did the Republican leaders do when they had a chance to increase our national defense almost three years ago? You would think from their present barrage of verbal pyrotechnics, that they rushed in to pass that bill, or that they even demanded a larger expansion of the navy.
>
> But, Ah! my friends, they were not in a national campaign for votes then.
>
> In those days they were trying to build a different kind of political fence.
>
> In those days they thought that the way to win votes was to represent the Administration as extravagant, indeed as hysterical and as manufacturing panics and inventing foreign dangers. . . .
>
> On the radio these Republican orators swing through the air with the greatest of ease; but the American people are not voting this year for the best trapeze performer. . . .
>
> Great Britain and a lot of other nations would never have received one ounce of help from us—if the decision had been left to Martin, Barton, and Fish. . . .

Papers, 1940, 504.

Mostly, as noted, he talked more about danger from aggressive enemies abroad than about political enemies at home. He accused the Republicans of hampering the build-up of defense. This his advisers thought was unwise. And it was certainly true that Americans were still strongly against running any risk of war. But the fact was that war was now in progress. The struggle was on between the democracies and the dictatorships. It was not yet the furious battle it later became and Americans would still have preferred to ignore it. Some isolationists invented a phrase for the situation. It was, they said, "a phony war." Britain and France, they said, were not fighting very hard; and we ourselves were not really in any danger. It was this isolationism that Franklin made the central issue of his campaign.

It was his thesis that Hitler was preparing not only to conquer Poland but all the rest of Europe—and then the rest of the world. He had begun this argument with the American people even before the campaign, even before his nomination. In May of 1940, for instance, he made his "50,000 plane" speech to the Congress. It was called this because, picturing the possibility of thousands of bombers over the American continent causing a devastation that might force surrender and subjection, he had gone on to ask for a vast expansion of our military forces—including 50,000 planes.

Lightning attacks, capable of destroying airplane factories and munition works hundreds of miles behind the lines, are a part of the new technique of modern war. . . .

The Atlantic and Pacific were reasonably adequate defense barriers when fleets under sail could move at five miles an hour. Even in those days it was possible by a sudden foray to burn our national capital. Later the oceans still gave strength to our defense when fleets and convoys propelled by steam could sail the oceans at fifteen or twenty miles an hour.

But the new element—air navigation—steps up the speed of possible attack to three hundred miles an hour.

Furthermore, it brings new possibilities of the use of nearer bases from which attacks on the American continents could be made. From the fiords of Greenland it is four hours by air to Newfoundland; five hours to Nova Scotia . . . and only six hours to New England.

The Azores are only 2,000 miles from parts of our Eastern seaboard and if Bermuda fell into hostile hands it would be a matter of less than three hours for bombers to reach our shores. . . .

Para, Brazil, is but four hours to Caracas; and Venezuela is but two-and-a-half hours to Cuba; and Cuba and the Canal Zone are two-and-a-quarter hours to Tampico; and Tampico is two-and-a-quarter hours to St. Louis, Kansas City and Omaha. . . .

Surely the developments of the past few weeks have made it clear to all our citizens that the possibility of attack on vital American zones . . . makes essential that we have the ability to meet those attacks. . . .

I should like to see this nation geared to turn out at least 50,000 planes a year. . . .

Papers, 1940, 202.

This seemed a fantastic number to commentators; and there were cries of scare-mongering. Franklin was so widely ridiculed that, even though he persisted, he felt forced for some time to be more cautious in what he said. Progress toward building defenses and even toward helping the Allies did not go nearly so fast as he feared was necessary.

The *official* neutrality of the United States had been abandoned in 1939 after a long and wearing fight. The Neutrality Act, passed a few years earlier, had been intended to make certain that the United States did not become involved; and isolationists hated to give it up. But Franklin won a hard fight to have it repealed; and this cleared the way for helping the Allies more openly. But the repealer had passed by a very narrow margin and the debate had been bitter.

Then in spring of 1940, and running through the election summer to fall, the aggressively savage intentions of the Nazis were made apparent. The Nazi war machine again went into action. First the Scandinavian countries were occupied; then the tanks and planes smashed through Belgium and Holland to outflank France's Maginot defense line. The British armies barely escaped through Dunkirk, leaving all their war material behind. France was conquered and occupied; and Britain's fall seemed imminent.

This was a complete confirmation of all that Franklin had been trying for years to make Americans understand. But even when they read about the Polish blitzkrieg, and listened to Franklin's impassioned warnings, there was more disposition to withdraw and huddle at home than to go out and fight. Thus, since Franklin had to get elected again if he was to bring the nation into the struggle, he often had to speak more moderately than he felt. He actually protested several times that he hoped and believed war could be avoided. Even as late as October, 1940, in a Boston speech, he said:

> Our objective is to keep any potential attacker as far from our continental shores as we possibly can.
> You here in New England know that well and can well visualize it. . . .
> Campaign orators seek to tear down the morale of the American people when they make false statements about the Army's equipment. I say to you that we are supplying our army with the best fighting equipment in all the world.
> I cannot help but feel that the most inexcusable, most unpatriotic misstatement about our army—a misstatement calculated to worry the mothers of the nation—is the brazen charge that men called to training will not be properly housed . . . very simply, and very honestly, I can give assurance to the mothers and fathers of America that each and every one of their boys will be well housed and well fed. . . .
> And while I am talking to you mothers and fathers, I give you one more assurance.
> I have said this before, but I shall say it again, and again, and again.
> Your boys are not going to be sent into any foreign wars.
> They are going into training to form a force so strong that, by its very existence, it will keep war away from our shores. . . .

Papers, 1940, 515, 517.

As election approached and the Nazis became more successful, Franklin felt able to take certain steps useful to the Allies even before the November election. The first peacetime draft was authorized; a deal was made to trade Britain forty old destroyers for bases in the Caribbean; the army and navy were enlarged; and progress was made in producing those 50,000 planes Franklin had spoken of and in training the men to fly them. This dismayed the professional politicians who judged that the country was still hesitant about involvement. What Franklin did was done of course in the name of *defense,* not of preparation for war. But it is doubtful that many people were fooled about this. By election day, it was plain enough to most Americans that there was no escape.

If Franklin's reassuring words and warlike actions seemed contradictory or hypocritical, the majority of the voters did not seem to hold it against him. On election day, they flocked to the polls. And that night, at Hyde Park, this was the atmosphere:

The night was warm for November, still and starless; on a flagpole above the portico the blue Presidential flag, with its shield, eagle and white stars, flapped listlessly. Hyde Park House was dark, the big green shutters swung snug to the front windows—from outside, not a crack of light showed from the library. Inside and out, the atmosphere was solemn, expectant, tense.

In station wagons and long shining limousines came people in evening clothes, neighbors and friends. Inside they assembled in the long, furniture-cluttered library, chatting quietly or sitting, hands in laps, listening to the radio chattering election returns.

Apart from his household, alone at the mahogany table in the family dining room, sat the master mathematician of U.S. politics. Outside the room's closed doors was expectant silence. Inside, Franklin Roosevelt worked calmly in the midst of the nerve-shattering, incessant clacking of three press tickers, loud in the empty room. Before him were large tally sheets with the States listed alphabetically across the top; a long row of freshly pointed pencils. His coat was off. His tie hung low under the unbuttoned collar of his soft shirt, but he had not rolled up his sleeves. His one companion was Marguerite ("Missy") LeHand, who snatched the latest "takes" from the thumping tickers, put them before the President without a word, as fast as he finished charting the latest tally. He enjoyed the job.

Occasionally, the doors slid softly open to admit Harry Hopkins or Judge Samuel I. Rosenman, but even the President's wife and mother kept out of this political sanctum in this sacred hour.

On the tally sheets his statistical election picture quickly took shape. Willkie's strength was inland, in the breadbasket States. Wherever land touched sea, Roosevelt was strong. The New England vote was a triumph for him: Maine went Republican only narrowly, and the President's vote in New England was even larger than in 1936.

But in the nation as a whole it was a different story. Everywhere Willkie did far better than Landon had done: for a time Republicans had hopes of Ohio, Illinois, Pennsylvania, all key States. But by 10 P.M. Roosevelt had 364 electoral votes, Willkie only 121, with the rest dubious. By 11 P.M. the President had telephoned Democratic Boss Ed Flynn that he was "very confident" of re-election.

At midnight New York was coming in fast and close, but Franklin Roosevelt, with all other big States in his bag, was in. At Hyde Park Harry Hopkins went out on the porch for a breath of air, happy to bursting point. The tension in the house had relaxed. Down the Albany Post Road tootled and whammed a fife, drum and bugle corps, behind them a straggling crowd of 500 villagers, carrying red railroad flares, and Squire Roosevelt of Hyde Park, first third-term President of the U.S., came out on the stone porch to joke with his friends. All day he had been jovially confident. That morning after voting (No. 292) at the town hall, accompanied by Wife Eleanor and Mother Sara, he had wisecracked with persistent New York *News* photographer Sammy Shuman. Shuman: "Will you wave at the trees, Mr. President?" Roosevelt: "Go climb a tree." Shuman: "Please." Roosevelt: "You know I never wave at trees unless they have leaves on them."

Now he said to the villagers: "I don't need to tell you that we face difficult days in this country, but I think you will find me in the future just exactly the same Franklin Roosevelt that you have known for a great many years."

The big-shouldered man who faced his neighbors leaning on the arm of son Franklin Jr. had won a third term. The vote had been sensationally large. If the election of 1940 had been a test of democracy, voters had met the test the only way they could: by voting 50,000,000 strong. Such an outpouring of ballots had never been seen in U.S. history. In New York City 95%-plus

Fala insists on going to the Inaugural; FDR tells him he must stay home, 1941

of the registered voters had voted—an almost unbelievable turn-out—a token of aroused feeling, of the bitterness of division among the electorate.

To every U.S. citizen the problem of national unity was just as serious as to the man jesting in the fizzling flare light on the Hyde Park porch. In the final count it appeared that there would be over 20,000,000 votes for Willkie and most of them were undoubtedly votes against Roosevelt. Besides a great victory Roosevelt also had the greatest vote of no confidence that any President ever received. On Franklin Roosevelt's brow rested something heavier than the laurels of political victory: on his big bland forehead lay a responsibility greater than any President's since Abraham Lincoln. Like Lincoln, he could and must quote Scripture: "A house divided against itself cannot stand."

Time, November 11, 1940.

Franklin regarded his victory as permission to go ahead with his opposition to the dictators and his aid to the Allies. And it did go a long way toward subduing the more active isolationists.

Between Christmas and New Year's Day he made one more powerful appeal for increased U.S. involvement in the war—this was the "Arsenal of Democracy" speech. He said:

> The British people and their allies are conducting an active war against an unholy alliance. Our own future security is dependent on the outcome of this fight. Our ability to "keep out of war" is going to be affected by that outcome.
>
> I make the direct statement that there is far less chance of the United States getting into war if we do all we can now to support the nations defending themselves against attack by the Axis than if we acquiesce in their defeat, submit tamely . . . and wait our turn to be the object of attack. . . .
>
> We must be the great arsenal of democracy. For us this is an emergency as serious as war itself. We must apply ourselves to our task with the same resolution, the same sense of urgency, the same spirit of patriotism and sacrifice as we would show if we were at war. . . .

Papers, 1940, 639, 640, 643.

But Americans were not yet wholly convinced. Even the election had not settled everything. Actual American participation in the war would require some greater shock, some further crisis, before it would be consented to by the people.

200

(28)

ON a morning late in November of 1940 the cruiser *Tuscaloosa* lay with stopped engines rocking in the swells of the Caribbean Sea. The sun was bright and the breeze gentle. Franklin, tired from the campaign just past, sat on the afterdeck, grateful for the rest he was having.

He was now within two months of being fifty-nine years old. He had stood the strain of the Presidency for nearly eight years and had just been re-elected to a third term. He had not found time for his usual Thanksgiving relaxation at Warm Springs and his exhaustion was evident. But he always came back at sea and he was reviving now. He needed to; there was no easy time ahead, only more strain and worry.

The Allies were in deep trouble. The British Isles had only the skimpiest of defenses. If there was a cross-Channel invasion being prepared, it was hard to see how it might be fended off. In the retreat from France most of the army's weapons had been left behind.

Franklin's reverie was interrupted by the landing of the daily mail plane beside the cruiser. Presently the newspapers and his letters were brought to him. He must spend the rest of the morning on the nation's business, as a President, wherever he is, must always do.

He did his duty by the documents he had to sign and laid aside a letter to be studied later. It was this message that Churchill said afterward was the most important paper he ever wrote. Franklin read it all thoroughly, then sat a long time considering what it had to say. It told the American President simply but eloquently that the situation of the British was now desperate; if the United States did not come to the rescue, invasion and occupation were inevitable.

In spite of his foreknowledge that Churchill would probably make such an appeal, he was deeply concerned. Unfortunately, what he could say in response was only that America could be depended on to sell arms and food. The time had not yet come when he could promise more.

Entering into his calculations, as he sat thinking, was also a recollection of troubled relations after World War I—caused by the debts the Allies could not pay. These debts had arisen when the British could no longer offer cash to American manufacturers because they had used up their funds.

The situation was much the same now. Franklin could offer the British assistance by allowing them to buy munitions. And how were they to be paid for? Unless some new scheme was devised there would be debts just as troublesome as the old ones had been. He thought loans would be approved because more and more people now saw that Britain was defending America as well as herself. But those debts after World War I had helped to bring on the Depression; what would happen if he approved more of them now?

During the rest of his vacation in southern waters Franklin kept considering how he could help the Allies without involving them in a vast debt. He began to formulate an idea. Why not loan the munitions themselves instead of money—munitions to be returned at some future time? Such a startling proposal had to be carefully prepared. He would have to persuade the Congress to approve. And it would all have to be done in the name of defense. But he thought it might be accepted.

Defense was a much overworked word in those months. When the Navy had to be strengthened and when the draft of young men for the Army had to be begun, it was defense that was always spoken of, never war. Now that the British were to be supplied from American fields and factories, it still had to be for defense. Americans still wanted to believe they were not preparing for war.

Time was running out for this evasiveness. Month by month

the American involvement became deeper. No one foresaw that within a year Pearl Harbor would have been attacked, and war would have been declared, but the conviction was gradually spreading that the Allies must be helped with a military force as well as munitions. The unhappy mood was evident even at the White House Christmas tree lighting ceremonies.

The master of the house stood bareheaded in the dusk before a huge red cedar on the browned turf of the elipse, at the south end of the Executive Mansion lawn, and listened to carols. Then he touched a silver switch, and ten thousand watts of hand-dipped stars officially opened the Christmas season for the good people of the United States.

A few minutes later, President Roosevelt, in a solemn but neighborly mood, told the 6,000 listeners before him, and the millions on the air: "Let us make this Christmas a merry one for the little children in our midst. For us of maturer years it cannot be merry."

U.S. News, January, 1941.

When Franklin got back to Washington from his cruise, he began his campaign for approval of what he spoke of in a press conference as "lend-lease." Follow, now, the presentation he made to the reporters, and imagine the headlines and feature stories in all the newspapers next day:

I don't think there is any particular news except possibly one thing that I think is worth my talking about. In the present world situation, of course, there is absolutely no doubt in the mind of a very overwhelming number of Americans that the best immediate defense of the United States is the success of Great Britain in defending itself. . . .

I go back to the idea that the one thing necessary for American national defense is additional productive facilities; and the more we increase those facilities—factories, shipbuilding ways, munitions plants and so on, the stronger American national defense is.

Orders from Great Britain are, therefore, a tremendous asset. There are several ways of encouraging it . . . we could lend the money to be spent over here . . . There is another . . . and that is a gift. I am not at all sure that is a necessity and I am not at all sure that Great Britain would care to have a gift from the taxpayers of the United States.

Well, there are other ways, and those ways are being explored. I have been at it now for three or four weeks. I will just put it this way, not as an exclusive alternative method but as one of several possible methods. . . .

It is possible for the United States to take over British orders . . . We have money enough to do it. And, thereupon, as to such portion of them as the military events of the future determine to be right and proper for us to allow to go to the other side, either lease or sell the materials, subject to mortgage, to the people on the other side. . . .

In other words, if you lend certain munitions and get the munitions back at the end of the war, if they . . . haven't been hurt you are all right; if they have been damaged or have been lost completely, it seems to me you come out pretty well if you have them replaced by the fellow to whom you have lent them. . . .

This last was not very convincing, perhaps; and certainly the deal was not made that way. What *was* convincing was the illustration he used:

Suppose my neighbor's home catches fire, and I have a length of garden hose four or five hundred feet away. If he can take my hose and connect it up with his hydrant, I may help him to put out his fire. Now what do I do? I don't say to him before that operation, "Neighbor, my garden hose cost me $15; you have to pay me $15 for it" . . . I don't want $15; I want my garden hose back after the fire is over. If it goes through the fire intact, he gives it back to me and thanks me for the use of it. But suppose it gets smashed up—gets holes in it—during the fire; we don't have to have too much formality about it, but I say to him "I was glad to lend you that hose; I see I can't use it any more . . ." He says, "All right, I will replace it." Now, if I get a nice garden hose back, I am in pretty good shape.

Papers, 1940, 604–607.

This, of course, was not the way it turned out. The British used up a good deal of American garden hose; and they replaced none of it. But conditions changed between the beginning and the end of 1941. What was arranged between mere friends was not appropriate for Allies in a war. In any case, when Churchill and Franklin met, they devised another formula which made the lease arrangement somewhat more realistic and equal. This was the gift or lease to the United States of military bases, mostly in the Caribbean and the Atlantic on the eastern approaches to the American coast. Whether Franklin believed that the United States would really get back its garden hose, or whether he knew very well that it would never be returned, is a matter of conjecture. No matter what his true feelings, his persuasion worked.

The Lend-Lease Bill passed the Congress, but not until March, 1941, and not until there had been a good deal of bitter talk. The weeks of delay were agonizing ones for Britain; but Churchill knew better than to press too hard. The President was doing his best.

In the "Arsenal of Democracy" speech Franklin had said that the way he had chosen was the way of least risk for the United States; there was, he said, no longer any reasonable alternative. And this was as far as he could go. He did not say, as he had during the recent campaign, that actual war might be avoided. And he met the argument of the opposition —that a negotiated peace was possible—by flatly denying the possibility, saying:

> The United States has no right or reason to talk of peace until the day shall come when there is clear intention on the part of the aggressor nations to abandon all thought of . . . conquering the world.

As soon as the act had been signed, he appointed Harry Hopkins its administrator, and supplies in vast quantities began to move overseas.

Franklin hoped that what was being done was enough and

would not be too late. Everything that had happened and everything that would happen during the spring and summer of 1941, indicated that the nation would presently be at war. But there were many still who hung back and, as any political leader must, Franklin respected this reluctance.

Some of his associates were making belligerent speeches against Hitler—Vice-President Wallace and Secretary Ickes, for instance—but the isolationists in the Senate and elsewhere were still watchful and ready to check any further moves. Then too, Franklin had strategic problems that were not easy to solve. American productivity was increasing, but it had not yet reached a satisfactory level. The draft of young men was going on, and training centers were being organized; but were not yet finished.

And there were the Japanese in the Pacific.

The Philippines were an American responsibility; General MacArthur was in command of the forces there. And Japan was carrying out the most rapid conquest in all history. The Dutch and British East Indies fell; China was overrun. Would the Philippines be next?

The Philippines would be hard to defend if they were attacked. It was best to treat the Japanese with extreme caution until the Navy was stronger, the armies trained, the British rehabilitation completed—and public opinion readier for war.

Franklin's temporizing annoyed his more impatient associates. And for him it was a difficult time. Robert E. Sherwood described the frustrations in the spring of 1941:

> During those days . . . Roosevelt spent a great deal of time in bed and rarely went to his office. He said that this was one of the most persistent colds he had ever had. One day, after long talk with him in his bedroom, I came out and said to Missy LeHand, "The President seems in fine shape to me. He didn't cough or sneeze or even blow his nose the whole time I was in there and he looked wonderfully well. What is really the matter with him? Missy smiled and said, "What he's suffering from is

a case of sheer exasperation." Indeed at the time he seemed to be exasperated with practically everyone. . . .

Very few people were allowed to see the President during those days. There were a lot of very nervous men in high places in Washington wondering what was the reason for his inaccessibility and, when the President should finally emerge from it, which way he would jump.

Roosevelt and Hopkins, Chap. XIII.

The whole outlook was abruptly changed in June when Hitler broke the treaty with the Russians that had made possible the conquest of France. With Western Europe conquered, Hitler felt strong enough to turn on his ally. This went against the rule forbidding a two-front war and was opposed by his military advisers; but Hitler's inflated ego would no longer tolerate any limit to his ambition.

It was a fatal mistake; and both Churchill and Franklin recognized this at once. There had long been hostility to Russia among the Western nations because of her communism. This, too, was a movement for world conquest and so a threat to other governments. It was felt that if Russia should ever be powerful enough to make the threat real, she would certainly undertake it. The unscrupulousness of the Communists had been shown by their treaty with Hitler. Nevertheless, with that treaty broken, Russia now became Hitler's enemy. This did not make her an ally of the democracies, but it did join them in the same cause. And it was only realistic to accept the advantage and make the most of it.

There was resistance to aiding Russia. The military advice coming to Franklin told him that the Germans would conquer Russia in a matter of weeks and there was nothing to gain by giving support. But neither Franklin nor Churchill believed this. They recalled how Napoleon had been defeated by distance and the Russian winter. They were convinced that the same thing would happen to Hitler.

It did. The Russians suffered defeat after defeat during the summer and fall; but when the cold came they still had not lost everything; and the Germans were still being resisted in the Russian interior.

By the time Hitler had learned the hopelessness of trying to conquer Russia, and had exhausted his armies in the attempt, there would be, Franklin was certain, new forces to oppose him in the West. They might—they would—be American as well as British. It was becoming plain now that the United States could not keep out of the war. At what moment this would happen, what incident would precipitate it, could not be foretold. But by the fall of 1941 it was only a question of such a moment and such an incident.

And Franklin was so certain of this that his mind turned to the peace that must follow the inevitable Allied struggle and Allied victory.

(29)

WAR was a certainty. Franklin was determined to make sure that the settlement following it was a lasting and just one. He envisioned a world organization for securing peace. And planning for that organization, even if it could only be established years in the future, could be started immediately.

Getting acceptance for such an organization would be a delicate matter, and strategy for it would have to be as carefully considered as the strategy for taking the country into war. The mistakes made by Wilson after the First World War, when he failed in persuading Americans to accept the League of Nations, would have to be avoided. But Franklin had lived during Wilson's time and understood the difficulties. He foresaw that when the peace was being made, the world would be a strange and dangerous one. Americans would still be reluctant to accept responsibilities beyond their own continent. But if one thing was clear and certain it was that the nations would be closely knit. Peoples would be situated so close to each other in time and place that they must learn to live together with moderation and tolerance.

The means for making them learn, for ensuring justice and equality for large nations and small, must be supplied by an agency especially devised to moderate ambitions, achieve compromises, and, if necessary, to discipline aggressors. The defeat of ambitious nationalists does not prevent them from becoming aggressive again as soon as they can. Only world pressure for peace, both moral and military, can stop them. And this pressure must be supplied by an organization of the nations of the world.

In the famous "Four Freedoms" message to Congress of January, 1941, Franklin envisioned a world in concert:

> In future days, which we seek to make secure, we look forward to a world founded upon four essential human freedoms.
>
> First is freedom of speech and expression—everywhere in the world.
>
> The second is the freedom of every person to worship God in his own way—everywhere in the world.
>
> The third is freedom from want—which, translated into world terms, means economic understandings which will secure to every nation a healthy peacetime life for its inhabitants—everywhere in the world.
>
> The fourth is freedom from fear—which, translated into world terms, means a world-wide reduction of armaments to such a point and in such a thorough fashion that no nation will be in a position to commit an act of physical aggression against any neighbor—anywhere in the world.

Papers, 1940, 672.

So in those last months of uneasy waiting, as the manufacture of lend-lease arms was speeded up, and as *matériel* began to move across the sea, Franklin was thinking too of ways to make certain that the war did not end as the last one had, in disillusion and futility.

The attention he gave to a world organization while the preparations for war were going on is certainly a justification for the care taken by the writers of our Constitution to make certain that the military should be subordinated to civil authority. It is for generals to win battles; but it is for the civil leaders to say what shall be done with the victory.

Franklin was wary of the many difficulties. The First World War had been defined by Wilson as the one "to make the world safe for democracy." But the European statesmen Wilson dealt with—Lloyd George of Britain, Clemenceau of France, and Orlando of Italy—had not only insisted on punishing Germany until she was prostrated, but on dividing up her territories as though they were so many counters in a game. The old empires centered in Europe—Austria-Hungary and Germany—had been broken up into several new nations on the principle of "the self-determination of peoples." But this caused as many troubles as it settled. There were still dissatisfied minorities; and the quarrels did not stop.

The Germans were still a proud people and Hitler had made a cause of their harsh treatment after World War I to rally them toward World War II. That another war came only a generation after the last, Franklin felt, was very largely because the United States had committed its forces to the Allied cause in 1917 without asking for guarantees. At the peace table Wilson had had to bargain hard to make the League of Nations a part of the Treaty of Versailles. He had got a sort of acceptance for it from the European leaders but only when he agreed to other provisions that were extravagantly vindictive. Defiance of these provisions had given Hitler his hold on the German people during the years of his rise.

Ever since that time Franklin had had in his mind the tragic picture of Wilson, home from the bargaining in Paris, exhausted, pleading for the acceptance of the agreements he had made, and suffering defeat by the "little group of willful men" in the Senate. They refused to ratify the treaty because, they said, it would involve America permanently in Europe's quarrels.

Our intervention in World War I had helped the British, French, and Italians to extend their own possessions at the expense of their enemies. But this was no gain for democracy or for the United States as a nation. Many Americans now felt it was far better to stay home and mind their own business, developing the nation and letting the Europeans fight among themselves if they must. This was dangerously close to saying that the war had been fought for no other reason than to defeat a hated enemy, not make a better world. Many glorified their own fighting ability but could not really say what the fighting had been about.

When Franklin had campaigned with Cox in 1920, he had

ardently defended the League as an instrument for keeping the peace—and the election had been lost disastrously. Now the nation was again on the verge of interfering in Europe. Would it again be merely to defeat a hated enemy? Or could Franklin succeed, where Wilson had failed, in defining aims and seeing that they were gained? The opponent this time was again Germany, but not the Germany of the Kaiser. Hitler was a more dangerous opponent because he seemed to be getting results more effectively than the Kaiser had or the democracy the Germans had tried to establish after World War I. Hitler, in fact, had overthrown the democratic Weimar Republic with the enthusiastic consent of the people.

Franklin had labored for years, as President, to explain the issue as he saw it, and as Wilson had seen it. Democracy could exist only if an organization to guarantee the peace were established. Otherwise the peaceable nations would always be at the mercy of whatever aggressive ones gained the strength to challenge international agreements or to attack their neighbors.

Franklin had resolved that he would only urge American participation in the war if the Allies would agree to a world organization projected beyond war into a new kind of peace —one made secure by an organization to ensure it.

Churchill was to be nearly as hard to deal with on this issue as the statesmen Wilson had dealt with in 1918–19. The English Prime Minister had always been an imperialist and had no intention of changing. Wilson had defined American aims in stirring pronouncements; but he had not insisted on commitment before war was declared. Franklin would not make that mistake. Also, he thought he could learn from Wilson's failure with the Senate. Franklin would try to avoid such a fight at home as Wilson had encountered. He would keep the Senate informed, admit its leaders to all the preliminary proceedings, and commit *them* to the peace as the nation was committed to war.

Late in the summer of 1940, with these thoughts in mind, and with the power of industrial America already boiling up to support the Allies, he arranged a meeting with Churchill —a dramatic meeting that would align America on the Allies' side, but would make certain, also, that the principles Franklin felt worth fighting for—the founding of a permanent peace— would be established as the aim of the allied effort.

The meeting was held at Argentia.

30

ON August 10, 1941, a heavy cruiser of the United States Navy crept cautiously through chilly Newfoundland mists and anchored in Argentia Bay. This was a name most Americans had never heard before; but from now on it would have a permanent place in the history books.

The big *Augusta* was making rendezvous with the *Prince of Wales,* pride of the British Navy. The one warship carried the President of the United States; the other carried the Prime Minister of Great Britain. Franklin no longer felt it unwise to meet Churchill and plan with him a common strategy. A British military staff was already in Washington; but this was not generally known. It was time now for a meeting of the civil leaders and a public pronouncement of aims.

Franklin had left Washington in early August in such secrecy as few Presidents have ever been able to manage. He had embarked first on the *Potomac,* the Presidential yacht, then transferred to the *Augusta* at sea. Newspapermen assigned to the White House had thought he was merely taking one of his recuperative voyages. Actually, during the next few days, after the ceremonious naval exchanges, the two Heads of State and their staffs would discuss what the two nations must now do together.

This meeting at sea ended all pretense that the United States was likely to escape actual involvement in the war. Opinion was turning rapidly in favor of the Allies. German ruthlessness was becoming more and more repulsive; the invasion of Belgium and France, and the atrocities carried out by occupation forces had aroused the same hostility as German savagery had aroused in 1917. There was also the inhuman determination to extinguish the whole Jewish population of Europe, now an explicit policy. This was genocide. What Franklin had been saying—that there was a real threat to Americans in this frightfulness—was beginning to be believed. It was more credible when American ships were sunk by submarines. After being safe since winning independence because of wide seas (and British seapower), Americans were learning that weapons from the air and under the sea had destroyed their traditional defenses. And effective new weapons were being used by a nation so ruthless that no end to its aggressions was foreseeable.

It had been a reluctant concession for the nation to become the "arsenal of democracy." But it would not be so hard from now on to support the British efforts. France had already fallen, and the British were obviously fighting for sheer survival. Franklin had more confidence now that public opinion was with him. At Argentia he came into the open as an Ally, not yet a formal one, but one ready, at least, to assist in planning the defeat of the common enemy.

But another purpose he had in meeting with Churchill was to exact a price for American participation. This time the stated aim of the war must be to unite the nations in a world organization that would make future aggressions impossible.

As a symbol of coming unity Harry Hopkins, as Lend-Lease Administrator, was on the British ship, a strange figure among the officers and statesmen. He had for a long time been very ill, and he seemed to be held together by sheer nerve. But Franklin depended on him, and had just sent him to Britain to find out for himself (and for Franklin) which of the Allies' needs were most urgent. Churchill had suggested that he come to the rendezvous on the *Prince of Wales*. His gaunt face and Midwestern speech were strange among the British. But all had agreed that no ally would be alien from now on. Hopkins was thus a symbol, an illustration of an eloquent passage in a Churchill speech to the British people. The affairs of the two nations, he said in the House of Commons, were

General Henri Giraud, FDR, General Charles de Gaulle, and
Winston Churchill at Casablanca, 1943

"being mixed up together." They would stay that way for the duration of the war—and go on that way for a long time to come.

This would, in fact, be only the first of many meetings between the Prime Minister and the President. Some of them would be in such places as Casablanca, Cairo, Teheran, Quebec, and Yalta; but most of them would be in the White House, where, for considerable periods of time, Churchill would live and work, recognizing that Washington was the real center of resistance to Hitler.

Franklin was well aware that Churchill's interest in the outcome of the war was narrower than his. In some ways it was one he could not approve.

For so imaginative a man, the Prime Minister was strangely stubborn about the changes that must be accepted as nationalism took belated hold on the minds of African and Asian peoples who were living in British dominions and colonies. Independence was just as fierce a sentiment for these nations as it had been for the North Americans who had broken away from Britain back in the eighteenth century.

The demand for self-government was part of Franklin's postwar problem. He foresaw that there would be dozens of new nations rising from the old empires—French, Dutch, and Portuguese, as well as British. It was probable that few of them would be really capable of self-government; but all would be determined to have it. And they would certainly be able to win. Their struggle, first for release from colonial ties, and then with each other in rivalry, might result in endless bickering, even in small wars. And any "brush fire" war might involve larger neighbors and endanger the world's peace. The postwar era would be inflammable as no other ever had; and it would involve the whole world.

Later generations might owe Franklin one debt more enormous than the arrest of depression, the systematizing of social security, or even victory in the war. If the United Nations could be accepted by his countrymen, and could gradually become a world government, one of the oldest dreams of mankind would be realized.

While he and Churchill planned with their advisers for winning the war, he put his own assistants to work outlining an international organization to take over when the war had been won. He actually began a campaign for peace very similar to that he had carried on for joining the war. Acceptance among Americans of membership in an international body would not come easily. They had rejected the League of Nations and many were still of the same mind.

What he would have to do first was to remind them what they were going to fight for—not just victory, but a permanent peace; not only to defeat totalitarians, but to make democracy safe. This campaign began with the statement issued after the Argentia meeting. It was called the Atlantic Charter:

August 14, 1941

The President of the United States and the Prime Minister, Mr. Chruchill, representing His Majesty's Government in the United Kingdom, having met together, deem it right to make known certain common principles in the national policies of their respective countries on which they base their hopes for a better future for the world.

First, their countries seek no aggrandizement, territorial or other.

Second, they desire to see no territorial changes that do not accord with the freely expressed wishes of the peoples concerned.

Third, they respect the right of all peoples to choose the form of government under which they will live; and they wish to see sovereign rights and self-government restored to those who have been forcibly deprived of them.

Fourth, they will endeavor, with due respect for their existing obligations, to further the enjoyment by all states, great or small, victor or vanquished, of access, on equal terms, to the trade and to the raw materials of the world which are needed for their economic prosperity.

Fifth, they desire to bring about the fullest collaboration between all nations in the economic field, with the object of securing, for all, improved labor standards, economic advancement, and social security.

Sixth, after the final destruction of the Nazi tyranny, they hope to see established a peace which will afford to all nations the means of dwelling in safety within their own boundaries, and which will afford assurance that all the men in all the lands may live out their lives in freedom from fear and want.

Seventh, such a peace should enable all men to traverse the high seas and oceans without hindrance.

Eighth, they believe that all of the nations of the world, for realistic as well as spiritual reasons, must come to the abandonment of the use of force. Since no future peace can be maintained if land, sea, or air armaments continue to be employed by nations which threaten, or may threaten, aggression outside their frontiers, they believe, pending the establishment of a wider and permanent system of general security, that the disarmament of such nations is essential. They will likewise aid and encourage all other practicable measures which will lighten for peace-loving peoples the crushing burden of armaments.

Papers, 1941, 314, 315.

It was significant that Franklin was able to win Churchill's consent to several of these clauses—such as that having to do with freedom of the seas, and freedom for small nations. These ran contrary to very old British policies. But Churchill was, of course, in a hopeless situation without American aid. He may have had such mental reservations as have eventually softened the commitment. But he did sign! And the already famous Four Freedoms were made the official intention of the two nations.

The charter was perhaps no more than a restatement of repeated American declarations—such as that in the preamble to the Constitution:

We the People of the United States, in Order to Form a More perfect Union, establish Justice, insure domestic Tranquility, provide for the common defence, promote the general Welfare, and secure the Blessings of Liberty to ourselves and our Posterity, do ordain and establish this Constitution for the United States of America.

But it had immense impact on minds confused by totalitarian propaganda, frightened by the prospect of war, and having still an active recollection of the Great Depression.

It was true that no declaration of this sort could really finish the argument still going on in the United States. The conviction that intervention must come was growing; but those hostile to Britain, those opposed altogether to intervention, and those who thought the totalitarians had the right idea, were still vocal. If Franklin, in his own mind, had declared war, the nation had not; and, as a good politician, he was entirely aware of it. Nor could he see any way to bring on the final decision. Tremendous efforts to increase production were being made; and military forces were being enlarged in the name of "defense." It was, nevertheless, a time of suspense.

It lasted until December 7, 1941.

(31)

IT was the Japanese who broke the American resistance to entering the war. As described by Robert Sherwood, this was Roosevelt's dilemma just before the Pearl Harbor attack:

> The Japanese were about to strike at British or Dutch possessions or both—and what could he do about it? The British and the Dutch were hopelessly unable to defend themselves and so were the exposed Dominions of Australia and New Zealand. Singapore might hold out for a while, but it and Manila would be made inoperative as bases with the Japanese in control of the air above them and the seas around them. Without formidable American intervention, the Japanese would be able to conquer and exploit an Empire, rich in resources, stretching from the Aleutian Islands to India or even the Middle East; and it was idle to assume, and Roosevelt knew it better than anyone else, that there could be any formidable American intervention without the full, final, and irrevocable plunging of the entire nation into war. . . .
>
> Even if Roosevelt, with the full use of the Democratic party whip, could compel the Congress to vote for war by a narrow margin after weeks or months of demoralizing debate, what degree of unity and fighting spirit could the American people achieve for the long and bloody effort that must be demanded of them. . . .
>
> There was just one thing that they [the Japanese] could do to get Roosevelt off the horns of the dilemma, and that is precisely what they did, in a manner so challenging, so insulting and enraging, that the . . . American people were instantly rendered unanimous.

Roosevelt and Hopkins, 429–430.

On the morning of December 7th the Japanese launched a bombing attack from the air. The planes flew in from undetected carriers to the north of the Hawaiian Islands. They caught many battleships concentrated at the Pearl Harbor naval base and sank most of them. Shore installations were wrecked and the loss of life was considerable.

Astonishment and indignation, followed by a furious determination to punish the attackers, spread over the whole country as the news became known. It was hard to believe the reports could be true; even the President could hardly credit them at first. The Japanese conquest of the South Pacific, reaching to the Dutch and British possessions, had been alarmingly successful. But that the United States would be attacked and challenged was unbelievable. Harry Hopkins wrote of the attack in a memorandum:

> I lunched with the President today at his desk in the Oval Room. We were talking about things far removed from the war when at about 1:40 Secretary Knox called and said that they had picked up a radio message from Honolulu from the Commander-in-Chief of our forces there advising all our stations that an air raid was on and that it was "no drill."
>
> I expressed the belief that there must be some mistake and that surely Japan would not attack in Honolulu.
>
> The President discussed at some length his effort to keep the country out of war and his earnest desire to complete his administration without war, but that if this action of Japan's were true it would take the matter entirely out of his hands, because the Japanese had made his decision for him.
>
> The President thought the report was probably true and thought it was just the kind of unexpected thing the Japanese would do, and that at the very time they were discussing peace in the Pacific they were plotting to overthrow it. . . .

Roosevelt and Hopkins, 431.

The Japanese were talking peace so persuasively at that time that the warnings of their belligerent actions in Asia and the Pacific had not been taken seriously enough. But after the attack on a Sunday morning the island of Oahu was prostrated. The warning system had failed, and the bombs and come down on a city and harbor completely unprepared.

In the crowded hours of that day, after the news came to Franklin and Hopkins in the Oval Room where they were "talking about things far removed from war," Franklin must have had some wonder whether he might not be held accountable. . . . It was only during the long hours of the afternoon that the full extent of the disaster developed. Not only the losses at Pearl Harbor grew with every report, but losses elsewhere as well. Hong Kong, Guam, Wake Island, Midway Island, were involved. . . . But the reaction was consistent with injured pride. What had given the Japanese the idea that they could affront Americans and get away with it? They would have to be punished. "Let's get down to it," everyone said. And Franklin's antennae very quickly registered the prevailing sentiment.

The Democratic Roosevelt, 589.

From Franklin's point of view there was only one compensation for the losses. The nation did at last come awake. If the Japanese had not attacked in this way, but had gone on conquering islands and nations in the South Pacific on the way to a junction with the Germans in Egypt, their ambitious plan might have succeeded.

As it was, what seemed at first a stunning success for them turned rapidly into failure. They had gone too far. Americans buckled down to work making good their losses in ships and planes. The counterattack did not come at once, of course, but when it did the punishment was a terrible one. Churchill, speaking before the U.S. Congress a month after the attack, expressed the British-American fury:

What kind of people do they think we are? Is it possible they do not realize we shall never cease to persevere against them until they have been taught a lesson which they and the world will never forget?

Once war had been declared Franklin assumed his constitutional duty as Commander-in-Chief. By the end of December, Churchill and his staff had come to Washington. And it was there that strategy was formulated and the whole direction of the war planned. The White House was the Allied headquarters.

First, theater commanders had to be chosen. Then it had to be decided where efforts should be concentrated and what priorities should be established. The two statesmen and their assistants began their labor at Christmas and went on working day and night into January. There were three commanders for the United States, besides Harry Hopkins who was given charge of the supply problem—General George Marshall for the Army, Admiral Ernest King for the Navy, and General Henry H. Arnold for the Air Force. Throughout the following years they would be depended on for command.

It was the suggestion of these chiefs of staff—with the concurrence of their British colleagues—that the first effort should be to defeat Germany meanwhile holding off the Japanese with such forces as could be spared. Since so many ships of the Pacific fleet had been lost at Pearl Harbor this might well be a period of retreat in the Pacific, even of humiliation. But this would have to be undergone. The Germans were the more dangerous enemy.

The ordeal of the Philippine and American soldiers besieged by the Japanese at Corregidor and Bataan was a cruel one. They could not be rescued or even reinforced; they could only be sacrificed. General MacArthur, being taken away in a submarine to organize new forces in Australia, could only say with a remnant of his customary arrogance, "I shall return."

That return would not be in time to prevent the horrors of the prison camps where men were beaten, starved, and allowed to suffer untended diseases; but his promise would be made good—in time.

This was not, however, until the war in Europe was on the way to being won and a Pacific island-hopping military force could be mounted. This would be 1944.

With Churchill at Casablanca, 1943

Such a convulsive effort to produce and deliver the materials of war as was made in 1942 and 1943 had never before been known. At first it was badly confused and there was much waste; but soon more order began to emerge. Camps for training sprang up everywhere; food was produced; munitions were manufactured; railways carried prodigious loads to the seaboards; and ships were built to carry the cargoes to the fighting ports.

Most of 1942 was needed for organization; and while the months passed, the nation was in danger from enemies on both sides. The holding operations of that year barely succeeded. It was a time of drawing together and of mutual effort. Even in the midst of the chaos following Pearl Harbor, twenty-six nations, whose representatives met in Washington, agreed on a United Nations Declaration. This constituted a pledge to pool resources and to make no separate peace with the enemy, and it was the first use of the name that would so long outlast the war as a union dedicated to peace. The Declaration was announced on New Year's Day, 1942:

> The Governments signatory hereto,
>
> Having subscribed to a common program of purposes and principles embodied in the Joint Declaration of the President of the United States of America and the Prime Minister of the United Kingdom. . . .
>
> Being convinced that complete victory over their enemies is essential to defend life, liberty, independence, and religious freedom, and to preserve human rights and justice in their own lands as well as in other lands, and that they are now engaged in a common struggle against savage and brutal forces seeking to subjugate the world, DECLARE
>
> (1) Each government pledges to employ its full resources military or economic, against those members of the tripartite pact or its adherents with which such Government is at war.
>
> (2) Each Government pledges itself to cooperate with the Governments signatory hereto and not to make separate armistice or peace with the enemies.
>
> The foregoing Declaration may be adhered to by other Nations which are, or which may be, rendering material assistance and contributions to the struggle for victory over Hitlerism.

Papers, 1942, 3, 4.

The Declaration was signed by the representatives of the

following countries, meeting in Washington: United States, United Kingdom, Union of Soviet Socialist Republics, China, Australia, Belgium, Canada, Costa Rica, Cuba, Czechoslovakia, Dominican Republic, Salvador, Greece, Guatemala, Haiti, Honduras, India, Luxembourg, Netherlands, New Zealand, Nicaragua, Norway, Panama, Poland, South Africa, Yugoslavia.

(32)

EVEN before America's formal entry into the war, the intensive study that produced the atomic bomb had started. We have spoken before of the revolution in living caused by electricity, telephone, automobile, radio, and similar inventions. The harnessing of nuclear power would open another era even more revolutionary, but although some may have suspected the potential of the atom for peaceful use as far back as 1939, the immediate scientific objective was to harness the atom in the cause of war.

It was obvious to Franklin from the moment he heard about it that the nuclear bomb could bring the war to an abrupt end; it would be the first truly mass-killing weapon in history. But neither he nor the scientists themselves knew how quickly the weapon could be developed. Many thought it would be developed too late to do any good. Others scoffed at the idea altogether.

The development of the [atom] bomb is of importance in illustrating Franklin's characteristic receptivity to what was novel. There is no better way to highlight this quality than to retell the famous remark of Admiral Leahy, Franklin's Chief of Staff. . . . The Admiral, when he heard about the bomb and who was working on it, remarked that he himself was an authority on explosives and that the idea of a superbomb was some damned professors' nonsense. . . .

It was not in direct answer to this remark, but it might well have been, that Professor Urey afterward pointed out something that Franklin instinctively knew. "No military man," Urey said, "ever invented a weapon."

The Democratic Roosevelt, 575.

Military science in Germany had, of course, progressed tremendously since the end of World War I. Even then German submarines had very nearly cut the United States off from the Allies. They were much improved now; and it was possible that this time they would absolutely dominate the seas. If they did, American help could not reach Europe. Even before Pearl Harbor the German fleet was growing fast and was imposing immense losses on ships attempting the Atlantic crossing.

The use of the Stuka planes to attack behind entrenchments, together with fast tanks to complete the enemy's disorganization, was a system that had already enabled the Germans to defeat France and overrun all of Western Europe. It was known that an invasion fleet of barges was being built and stored in harbors across the Channel from England; and smashing bombardment from the air had been countered and eventually stopped only by the individual heroism of English fliers using the tiny Spitfire plane. But other attacks would come; and if the submarines could keep American ships off the seas, the Allies would this time be defeated.

Thus the problem faced by Franklin and Churchill as they began to plan together in 1941 was not primarily the rapid development of the nuclear weapon, but rather the catching up with the Germans in all phases of military science. First, there was the question of keeping supply routes open; then of getting the American Army into battle. Could ships be built to travel so fast that German submarines could not sink them? It was not certain that they could. A system of convoys would help; but destroyer escorts could not guarantee that many ships would not be sunk.

Up to this time, the new ideas, the innovations had originated with the other side. Courage and industry were all very well; but the fast tanks, the bombers, and the submarines so far had the best of it. It was a time to look for other possibilities; and some of them were brought to Franklin's attention by civilians who knew what military men did not—that there were many new possibilities, still in testing stages, that might make tremendous differences in the battles of the future.

This need is what caused Franklin to accept eagerly the suggestion that British and American scientists might be enlisted and their work directed to the winning of the war. He was assured that concentrated effort might quickly produce startling results in aeronautics, in radar, in sonar, and especially in nuclear fission. Airplanes might be improved, defenses against submarines might really become effective, and —just possibly—there might be developed the weapon that would end all weapons because of its incredible destructiveness.

A small group for exploring the possibility of controlled nuclear fission had been set up as early as 1939. By 1940 Franklin had known that what had been suggested was feasible.

A National Defense Research Committee was formed and began to contract with various universities for carrying on parts of a systematized development program. Controlled fission first took place in an improvised laboratory at the University of Chicago.

The work then came under military direction and, rechristened the Manhattan Project, went on until the first bomb was actually tested at Alamogordo in 1945.

Almost from the first, and with growing concern, the scientists anticipated a race with the German scientists. Much of the groundwork had been laid in German laboratories, and in fact, it was two Germans who achieved the first reaction which pointed directly to Alamogordo. Otto Hahn and Friedrich Strassmann, bombarding uranium with neutrons, had produced barium. Speculating on this, two Jewish exiles in Denmark, Lise Meitner and her nephew, Otto Frisch, guessed that what had happened was that the nucleus had split. Nils Bohr, the noted Dane, carried this news to a conference on theoretical physics held at the Carnegie Institution in Washington. . . . There was

With Stalin at Teheran, 1943

great excitement in the scientific world. . . . This excitement gradually focused in later work at Chicago, then at Los Alamos, and at Oak Ridge.

The Democratic Roosevelt, 574.

The names associated with this work belong to an imperishable roster—Fermi, Szilard, Compton, Wigner, Bethe, Bohr, and others. Most of these were not of American origin; some were German, some were Hungarian, some were Danes; and what they knew, the enemy scientists must also know. One of the greatest worries of the next few years was the fear that the Germans would be the first to create the terrible weapon that nuclear fission would make possible.

As it turned out, Hitler decided against further work on the fission bomb. He thought it could not be developed in time and preferred to push other possibilities. One of these, the rocket, did cause grave damage to London in a blitz more awful than the aerial one of 1940. And when the Allies invaded the Continent in 1944 they found installations being built that might in a matter of months have made the Channel crossing impossible by destroying the British bases.

In a sense it was a war of scientists. The Japanese retribution was prepared by the effrontery that awakened America. The Germans suffered equally from their incredibly foolish treatment of the intellectuals who might have prepared the bomb ahead of the Allies. Instead, they reduced the universities to Nazi training centers. They insisted on telling scientists what results to achieve. They drove out or exterminated all the Jewish intellectuals, such as Einstein and Lise Meitner.

The Germans were defeated before the bomb had become operational; but the submarines were checked by sonar and radar and the Luftwaffe was eventually driven from the skies by superior Allied planes.

In 1941, when the British and Americans first began to work together on plans, the German war machine had a preponderance on land and seemed about to command the seas. And the Japanese were still pouring in millions of troops across China and into Southeast Asia.

It was a fearsome prospect.

IT is not the intention here to review the events of World War II in detail. They are described and analyzed in other volumes, and no recapitulation here could possibly give them the importance and scope they actually had. What must be said, however, is that the war and the peace to follow were the first concerns of Franklin's third administration and the few months of his fourth. Other issues seemed at the time, and seem in retrospect, far less important.

Franklin addressed a joint session of the Congress on the day after Pearl Harbor, asking for a Declaration of War, something only the Congress has the constitutional power to grant. He called December 7th "a day of infamy," thus emphasizing the treachery of the attack—and the country agreed.

It was well known that there were Japanese envoys in Washington to negotiate differences between the two governments. They had talked of peace even while the Imperial fleet was steaming toward Hawaii with orders for the bombing. This duplicity added to the anger everyone felt, and swept away all hesitation about getting into the war.

The Congress acted at once, and along with the Declaration voted ample funds for the vast enlargement of the military forces that must be made at urgent speed.

The emergency brought President and Congress together in one purpose, something that had not happened since the early days of the New Deal.

But the good relations did not last. Beginning a few weeks later, Franklin began to ask for the restraints and regulations on business and labor (no strikes, fair prices, fair wage levels, etc.) necessary in wartime, and the Congress again balked, showing the familiar determination to give and receive favors regardless of the national interest.

There were feverish efforts on the part of businessmen to take advantage of the tremendous expansion of industry that could be seen coming. War contracts are always enormously profitable. There was hurry amounting to hysteria; and not too much attention was given to the price paid for supplies. With huge profits in prospect, businessmen who hoped to share in them swarmed into Washington, not only milling about the military centers, but haunting Congressmen's offices as well. If a contract was to be had, each Congressman wanted it for his district. If he could get it for a constituent the favor would be returned when he needed support during his next campaign.

Experienced as Franklin was by now, he counted on a longer period of freedom to concentrate on military matters than he actually was given. As a matter of fact, by the time the Congressional elections of 1942 came around, he and the Congress were having more serious quarrels than ever before. The Congressmen refused to let the war make any difference in their concern for local interests; Franklin, being terribly pressed by all the problems presented by organization for war, was impatient with their demands. Several times he rebuked them openly. But this only added to their hostility.

The year 1942 was the low point in our nation's fortunes:

> The year was the one in all recent history which ran closest to the margins of national disaster. It was a narrow escape, far narrower than most Americans realized as they were going through it. The Japanese were denied Australia by the inconclusive battle of the Coral Sea; and they were turned back at Midway from a western thrust. But these were checks only and they were on the far west and south reaches of the enormous fan spreading down across the Pacific. The British and Dutch Empires in the southeast were gone, and the Philippines had surrendered. . . .

The Democratic Roosevelt, 598.

At first the Navy could do no more than make frantic efforts to rebuild its strength after the disaster of Pearl Harbor. The Japanese for some reason did not follow up their advantage with an attack on West Coast harbors, and the Germans did not attack Puerto Rico, the Panama Canal, or even the Atlantic ports. But they might have; and there was something like panic for fear they would. This was something Franklin had to deal with too. But he had little to work with as Commander-in-Chief for nearly two years.

There were those who did not scruple to take advantage of the national hysteria. It was at this time, for instance, that Franklin consented, on recommendation of the military, to send the descendants of Japanese immigrants to concentration camps. Their property was seized, and generally there was a disgraceful giving way to prejudice and fear, something to be explained only as reaction to the sudden danger of attack. There was some disposition to treat people of German origin in the same way; but they were more widely scattered and more integrated into their communities than the Japanese. The impulse to find a punishable enemy in time of frustration did not last long, but it was ugly while it lasted.

Franklin did somehow drive ahead through the confusions, mistakes, and quarrels of the early months of war without serious check. As soon as he was certain that the disaster of Pearl Harbor would result in national determination to fight, he was reassured. The will of the people was strong, even though the Congress seemed to have its mind on everything but war. The Congress made efforts to ensure that certain private interests—large growers of cotton, wheat, and live stock, munitions producers, oil interests, and others—made tremendous profits; also that no more New Deal legislation was approved. But Franklin did somehow get on with his job as Commander-in-Chief.

In 1942 he was given further warning of trouble to come: The Republicans gained forty-seven seats in the House and ten in the Senate. This gave them new courage rather than restraint; and the strengthened condition of Republicans and

Democratic conservatives made it even harder to maintain regulations for allocating raw materials to the war effort. It looked as though the early defeats and the general lack of coordination in production would cost the Democrats the Presidential election two years later.

But slowly the Navy was rebuilt, the Army was expanded, and the immense political strength of the nation began to be felt. If the conduct of the war is surveyed from the United Nations Declaration early in 1942 to its ending in 1945, it can be seen that Franklin had been right when he initially judged that an Allied victory was certain from the first.

When Hitler invaded Russia on June 22, 1941, he became all the more certain. The Russians suffered terribly in those first days—the German battle plan, in fact, counted on Russian resistance for no more than three months. But the Russians slowly gathered strength; by the beginning of winter, they had rallied and held, and by December 29th had counterattacked along the Moscow front. And while the Germans were thus engaged in the east, the Allies in the west had had time to prepare and regroup their forces.

In late 1942 it began to be apparent too that the Japanese had overextended themselves. Like the Germans in Russia, they found that the size of the area they attempted to conquer —in their case, the entire Pacific—was far beyond their capability, and they were soon forced to go on the defensive.

When the American Navy's losses at Pearl Harbor had been made up by frantic construction of new ships, and these had been deployed, the Japanese could not match the expanding power of the nation they had challenged. They sometimes won battles, but they were inevitably worn down in the long struggle. They lost ship after ship, plane after plane, until finally they had left neither navy, merchant marine, nor aircraft. The United States had losses too; but the capacity to build kept the fleets growing until finally their power was overwhelming.

After the Russians stopped the Germans just outside Leningrad and Moscow, winter paralyzed the Germans (much as it had Napoleon) and, with their supplies drastically cut, they were forced into a defensive position. The Allies made enormous efforts to send supplies by both the northern and southern routes—through the Arctic Sea to Archangel and up across Persia. Mere passage through the dark and stormy northern seas was bad enough, but the submarines that hung on the flanks of the convoys sank a fearful percentage of the ships. And until roads and railways could be built, the long routes across Persia were not very useful. But by dint of immense sacrificial efforts, enough supplies got through so that by spring the Russians were able to turn back the exhausted Wehrmacht. From then on the Germans would be on the defensive.

Despite the Allied efforts, Stalin, the Russian Premier and Commander, was never satisfied that the British and Americans were doing all they could. He pressed them continually to open a second front in Europe to relieve the pressure on his lines. This meant crossing the English Channel, and the Germans were now in control of the whole coast. There would be enormous losses, and the attack would fail unless careful preparations were made.

The British and American commanders argued a good deal about this possibility. At first the Americans believed an invasion could be staged in 1942. A more realistic appraisal put this off until 1943; and actually it did not take place until 1944.

If Churchill had had his way the cross-Channel invasion might not have taken place at all. His view of the grand strategy called for an invasion from the south rather than across the Channel. He spoke of the "soft underbelly" of Europe, and argued that this was the least difficult invasion route. What he had in mind, the Americans believed, was not so much an attack on the Germans as cutting off the Russians in their pursuit of the Germans westward. He dreaded their presence in Western Europe.

It was as a compromise that the first large-scale undertaking was a landing in North Africa, leading to the surrender of the elite German Afrika Korps. It was conceived by Allied planners in 1943 that if the coast opposite Europe was occupied, the underbelly would be even more vulnerable and the German defense would have to be thinned out to defend it. This dispersion of forces would weaken their effort elsewhere.

This was the first experience of the new American Army with modern operations. At first it was frustrated by the hardened desert armies of the enemy. But it learned rapidly, and fought its way east to meet the British coming from Egypt in the west. Within a year the conquest had been completed. Forces had been freed to cross into Sicily and begin an attack on Italy.

The Italian campaign was a grim one, lasting almost until the end of the war. The Allied invasion of Sicily under the over-all command of General Eisenhower, on July 10, 1943, so demoralized the Italian people that Mussolini was deposed as Premier in July and his successor, Marshal Pietro Badoglio, surrendered the Italian armies unconditionally on September 8th. But the Germans kept fighting in northern Italy, giving ground grudgingly. They did not surrender their Italian forces until May 2, 1945.

Meanwhile, General Eisenhower had been assigned to planning in England for the cross-Channel invasion to take place as soon as the immense armies, the flotillas of supplies, and all other material essential to success could be organized.

D-Day—the Allied invasion of Normandy—took place on June 6, 1944. Hundreds of thousands of troops, carried in 4,000 ships and accompanied by hundreds of planes, launched the attack between Cherbourg and Le Havre—and encountered fearsome German resistance. But after weeks of vicious fighting, the beachhead was secured, and on July 26th an American armored column broke through the German lines. The reconquest of France—and the defeat of Germany—was only a matter of time.

(**34**)

WE have described the meetings between Franklin and Winston Churchill which were to play an important part in the Allied strategy at the beginning of the war. Such conferences were held from time to time throughout the war as conditions changed and new moves—soon offensive rather than defensive—had to be designed.

One of the most important of these was at Casablanca in the beginning of January, 1943, just after French Africa had been made secure. It was here that the invasion of Sicily was planned, along with plans for the course of British-American action against the Japanese. It was here, too, that Franklin laid down his policy of unconditional surrender for the enemy, a policy later harshly criticized, by liberals in particular, on the grounds that it hardened the enemy's determination.

Perhaps the most significant influence at Casablanca was the man who wasn't there—Josef Stalin. Still bitter because the second front in Europe had not yet been undertaken, he implied that until the Americans and English were as busy fighting as the Russians, they would not be entitled to equality with the Russians.

Still, it was obvious that a meeting of the Big Three would have to be held, and Stalin did come to one in Teheran some eleven months later. At this meeting Franklin had two firm goals in mind: the promise of Russian support against the Japanese once the war in Europe had ended; and the promise of Russian and British support for a world organization for peace. For his part Stalin wanted further assurances that a cross-Channel invasion was indeed being prepared without further delay, and that Germany would be completely dis-

With General Dwight D. Eisenhower on the way to Malta, 1943

Christmas Eve at Hyde Park, 1943

armed to a point where it could never constitute a threat to Russia again.

From Franklin's point of view, the meeting went as he had hoped. Stalin readily agreed to join in the fight against the Japanese, and while he did not seem particularly excited about the idea of a world peace organization, he asked Franklin intelligent questions about it and at least evinced more interest than Churchill who, still the old imperialist, had no enthusiasm for the idea.

Roosevelt left Teheran visibly elated. He had not had much encouragement about a permanent world organization, and nothing definite had been settled, but he had at least received assurance that there would be no strenuous opposition by either Britain or Russia. There was no longer any doubt that the war in Europe would be won by the Allies and, with Russian support, the successful end of the war against the Japanese was in sight.

Despite his elation, however, Franklin returned from Teheran in a dangerously exhausted state. He had developed a racking bronchial cough which he could not shake, and his former lighthearted manner with associates had disappeared. He spoke movingly to the nation of his vision of the development of a United Nations once the war ended, but his relations with the Congress had still further deteriorated. Congressmen were so influenced by pressure groups and special interests that virtually no legislation of general public benefit could be passed. In fact, the only important act passed that spring was the "G.I. Bill," allowing returning servicemen education and other benefits at government expense. Franklin spoke to the Congress in a way he had never done before:

> . . . a noisy minority maintains an uproar of demands for special favors for special groups. There are pests who swarm through the lobbies of the Congress and the cocktail bars of Washington, representing these special groups as opposed to the nation as a whole. They have come to look upon the war as primarily a chance to make profits for themselves at the ex-

pense of their neighbors—profits in money or political or social preferment.

The Democratic Roosevelt, 613.

In early spring his health was in such a precarious state that his physician insisted on his taking a long vacation, and he went South for a few weeks. Immediately, his critics, both Democratic and Republican, insinuated that he was dangerously ill and unfit for the Presidency; but he seemed to recover much of his buoyancy and soon the insinuations slackened.

There was much discussion about the chances of a fourth term, but this too abated as, first, the fall of Rome to the Allied army and then D-Day itself turned the nation's attention to the war.

Nevertheless, politics became a main consideration of that summer. The Republicans nominated Thomas E. Dewey, the former district attorney, now Governor of New York. He was, Franklin said afterward, the most irresponsible opponent he had ever had. Dewey's attack centered on the delays and inefficiencies of the past two years. He claimed that too often the war had been badly run and national affairs mismanaged. This last was in some respects true. If many of the troubles were the result of Congressional opposition to Franklin's programs, Franklin could still not escape responsibility altogether. In addition, he had to overcome the prejudice that lingered even in his own party against more than two terms. This had caused the defection of Vice-President Garner and party chairman Farley in 1940. In 1944, too, Franklin did not have the harmony that a President seeking renomination can usually count on.

Franklin stayed away from the Democratic nominating convention. The city bosses were still with him, as they had been in 1940. So were the labor leaders, both groups unable to resist Franklin's popularity among those who had received

New Deal assistance. Members of their organizations knew very well to whom they owed their new benefits.

But in order to placate the bosses, Roosevelt allowed his Vice-President, Henry Wallace, to be displaced by Harry S Truman. Truman was the product of Kansas City's Pendergast machine. He had been a Senator for ten years and had pleased Franklin by managing a Senatorial investigation into the conduct of the war so that it was helpful rather than embarrassing. Franklin knew he would have to leave the campaign mostly to the bosses, and they told him Truman would make it easier to win. He allowed them to have their way, a fateful decision: unknown to any of those involved, they had chosen a future President.

As the campaign progressed, Dewey's attacks grew more violent. Franklin afterward confessed to his son James that Dewey "made me a little mad" with his claims that he was the better internationalist. He was sure that if Dewey won, the Republicans would do to the plan for a United Nations what they did to Wilson's League of Nations in 1918. He did not make many speeches, but those he did make (such as the famous "Fala" speech in which he sarcastically poked fun at the Republicans for attacking his dog) had much of the old fire in them.

Nevertheless, he entered the campaign reluctantly. He felt that what was at stake in those summer months was so serious for the people of the whole world that it ought not be made the hazard in a scramble for political office. And actually, he entered the campaign not so much because of Dewey's shrill attacks as because he sensed in the nation itself a reluctance to accept wartime restrictions and difficulties now that the war was almost over. He was afraid that the discipline and self-sacrifice Americans had evidenced throughout the war would break down with the war's end and that, in their desire to be rid of responsibility, they would refuse to support further international involvement. No one but himself, he felt, could see to it that they did not do again what had been done in 1918.

With Harry Truman and Henry Wallace right after the election, 1944

So he campaigned. And, since the Republicans had to admit that the war *was* being won, and that some sort of organization for peace was a necessity, he was re-elected.

The electoral vote was 432 to 99, not very different from that of 1940. But the partisanship of Dewey's speeches and a certain increase in the popular vote for the Republicans made Franklin fearful that his great project might be endangered in spite of the victory. He would have to use the utmost care to avoid rejection by the Senate of his United Nations as Wilson's League had been rejected there.

Time magazine described election day, 1944:

. . . Franklin Roosevelt slept late, set out at noon in the warm sunshine for the oakbeamed town hall at Hyde Park. There, at the polls, where he gave his occupation to Inspector Mildred M. Todd as "tree-grower," he enthusiastically accepted a piece of candy from Miss Todd, entered the booth munching.

There was a light Hyde Park supper of scrambled eggs, his "lucky dish." Then the President sat down to the old game at which he is expert—tabulating election returns. Supper dishes and cloth were whisked away; tally sheets and sharpened pencils were laid on the green felt cover. The big radio, provided by NBC, began to announce returns. Secretary Grace Tully and Mrs. Ruth Rumelt, Steve Early's A.P. and U.P. tickers. Around the big table, individual state scores were kept by the President's intimates: Henry Morgenthau, Admiral Leahy, Steve Early, Samuel Rosenman, Robert Sherwood. As "managing editor," the President assembled the totals.

Vice Admiral Ross T. McIntyre, the President's personal physician, hovered close; he would not leave, he said, unless or until. the returns moved substantially in F. D. R.'s favor. (He left just before 11 P.M.) At 11:15 came the dull thump of a base drum and the shrill tootle of fifes, and the usual torchlight parade of neighbors milled up the circular driveway.

The President was wheeled out on the porch by Valet Arthur Prettyman. Mr. Roosevelt remarked playfully that on the basis of partial returns it appeared that returns were partial to Hyde Park. In high good humor, grinning at the battery of photographers, he noted several children in the branches of one of the trees, and recalled how he had climbed the very same tree as a child to escape discipline. From that tree, he said, he saw his first torchlight parade from the village, at the time of Cleveland's election in 1892. "I got out of bed to come downstairs in an old-fashioned nightshirt—wrapped in a big buffalo robe."

Then the President went back into the house. Reporters were folding up their notebooks when Eleanor Roosevelt popped up in the door and remarked in a stage whisper to a group of chattering Vassar girls: "The President thinks the election is won."

Time, November, 1944.

246

(35)

AS the election approached, American initiative in the Pacific gained momentum. When troops could be spared from the European theater, and as naval victories opened the way, a strategy of "island hopping" was adopted. This meant that only a few of the larger islands need be captured; the smaller ones could be ignored. In this way many of the Japanese army units were stranded on islands with no way to get supplies or assistance. They never really came into the battles as the Americans forced their way across the Pacific.

Finally an attack could be made on the Philippines. The Japanese had to throw all their remaining naval power into the defense of the approaches to Leyte Gulf. The battles of October, 1944, were the largest naval battles in history. When they were finished the Japanese Navy's power to resist was destroyed. General MacArthur was then able to land and begin the reduction of the last Japanese defenses in the Pacific. He had returned as he had promised.

The vast Japanese conquests in the Pacific were by now virtually gone, their navies were helpless, and their armies had lost their lines of supply and communication. Shortly there would remain for the Americans only the home islands to capture. With that done the Japanese armies deployed in China, Burma, Indochina, and all across the South Pacific, would have no alternative but to surrender.

Actually, of course, the war against Japan ended sooner than it might have because of the Atomic Bomb. But the first A-Bomb was not dropped until August 6, 1945, and the decision to use it was spared Franklin. He had died in April. Perhaps it is futile to argue that he would have decided against its use; but it is true to say that his concern had been only to develop the bomb before the Nazis did, and it is possible that the consequences of using it, when the war was practically over, might have caused him to regret its use. It was argued by President Truman, his successor, that the bomb saved a million American lives (the estimated cost of capturing the home islands). At any rate, five days after the second bomb was dropped on Nagasaki on August 9, the Japanese did surrender (although the formalities were not concluded until September 2).

It was afterward disclosed that the Japanese had been trying for six months or more through intermediaries to find a way to end resistance. They insisted only that the position of the Emperor should be protected—a condition granted in the final terms. Why these approaches were rejected by President Truman, no one knows.

On the other side of the world, the war had been over for some months. In December, 1944, the Germans launched a desperate counterattack in an effort to reverse the trend of the war—the Battle of the Bulge. The Americans were driven back at first but the Germans no longer had the power to meet the reinforcements at General Eisenhower's disposal, and by Christmas the attack had clearly failed. In January the Germans lost all the territory they had regained—at the cost of over 200,000 dead or taken prisoner. It was their last effort. The Allies' relentless drive resumed. Presently the Russian armies took Berlin, Hitler committed suicide in his bomb shelter; and on May 7, 1945, the unconditional surrender Franklin had insisted upon, but was never to see, took place.

In this last war year, at the beginning of February, Franklin had set out for a final Big Three conference—at Yalta, in the Crimea. Here, as in Teheran, his purposes were first to gain Russian support of the war against Japan, but also to establish final acceptance for a permanent United Nations Organization.

In order to achieve his aims, he had to make concessions.

Churchill was still pursuing old British imperialist interests and Stalin was no more enthusiastic than he had been at Teheran. He too showed the imperial drive beneath the Communist cover. He meant to set up satellites in Eastern Europe and get access to the warm-water ports of the south, including control of the Dardenelles. Nevertheless, Franklin got what he wanted most: Russian support in Asia, and an agreement on a firm plan for a United Nations.

The plan had been carefully considered at home beforehand. A group assigned to drafting had been at work in the Department of State since the beginning of the war, under Franklin's close supervision. He knew that he must have support at home, and he had been careful to consult with influential legislators as the plan took shape, asking their advice at every stage of its development. When, at Yalta, he opened the question, he had approval back home; and when he left Yalta, with Churchill's and Stalin's definite promise of a meeting in San Francisco on April 25, 1945, to establish a permanent organization, he was sure that the meeting would take place and would have the support necessary for the ratification of a treaty including a United Nations.

Churchill remained indifferent; Stalin was fearful that small nations would be given enough power to start trouble that the large nations would have to finish. But Franklin, too, had thought of this and was able to satisfy the Russian on this point.

The original conception for the United Nations, growing out of the conception for the League of Nations, had been considerably modified by those who had drafted the final proposal. It had been simple, The Big Powers—five, including France, at Franklin's insistence, and China, because Franklin could not see how a world organization could leave out such a large proportion of its people—were to accept the duty of keeping peace among themselves and enforcing it on others. If they agreed to arbitrate their differences, and to pool their police forces, world order could be assured.

This seemed undemocratic to the group in the State Department who did the drafting. They believed in self-determination, and, in effect, equality among small nations and large alike. This was exactly what Franklin had seen as the League weakness. With so many unequal nations having an equal voice, no nation could ever be disciplined. Opposition to any action would always be stronger than any proposal for suppression of disorder.

Franklin was brought to consider a compromise in the end. There would be an Assembly where the votes would be equal for all nations; but it would be only a debating body. A small Security Council would make all real decisions, and the Big Five would have permanent membership. There would be three other members—a minority from the smaller nations. These members would rotate, that is, they would have temporary membership.

Franklin finally felt that he had, in the concept of the Security Council, substantially what he wanted. Any resolution passed there must have seven affirmative votes, and all the Big Five must vote for it; the small nations would not be too powerful.

Franklin was able to convince Stalin that this was so; and he left Yalta feeling that the organization was assured of Russian support. In order to ensure American acceptance, he announced immediately the delegates he would name. It was a carefully considered bi-partisan delegation, including three influential Republicans (Senator Vanderburg of Michigan, former Governor Stassen of Minnesota, and Congressman Eaton) and four influential Democrats (Secretary of State Stettinius, former Secretary Hull, Senator Connally of Texas, and Congressman Bloom of New York). He added Dean Gildersleeve of Barnard College, presumably to gain women's support.

When he returned to America with the Yalta agreement, his situation was quite different from that of Wilson when he returned from Paris in 1919. Prominent Senators had been consulted; the American delegation was generally approved; and the whole proposal now aroused none of the partisan

Arrival at Crimea, 1945

The Big Three at Yalta, 1945

hostility that had kept the United States out of the League in 1918.

This was a triumph; but in other respects, the country was in turmoil. The Congress was refusing to accept any more recommendations from Franklin and was insisting that the military organization be dismantled as rapidly as possible. Demand, soon to grow irresistible, was already strident for the immediate return of the troops from overseas.

Franklin saw that there would still be a need for soldiers. The enemy countries must be occupied, new governments must be established where the armies had been fighting and someone must see to it that these new governments were democratic. But the Congress was deaf to these warnings. They insisted the troops be brought home.

These problems were serious; but if the United Nations became a living organization they were minor worries in such a troubled world.

On his return, Franklin addressed the hostile Congress at once. He was ill now with what would be his final illness. He could not stand. He spoke from his chair:

> ... For the second time, in the lives of most of us, this generation is face to face with the objective of preventing wars. To meet that objective, the nations of the world will either have a plan or they will not. The groundwork of a plan has now been furnished and has been submitted to humanity for discussion and decision. No plan is perfect. Whatever is adopted at San Francisco will doubtless have to be amended time and again over the years, just as our own Constitution has been. No one can say exactly how long any plan will last. Peace can endure only so long as humanity really insists upon it, and is willing to work for it, and sacrifice for it.
>
> ... Twenty-five years ago, American fighting men looked to the statesmen of the world to finish the work of peace for which they fought and suffered. We failed them. We failed them then. We cannot fail them again, and expect the world to survive.
>
> I think the Crimea Conference was a successful effort by the three leading nations to find a common ground for peace. It

spells—and it ought to spell—the end of the system of uni-
lateral action, exclusive alliances, and spheres of influence, and
balances of power and all the other expedients which have been
tried for centuries and have always failed.

We propose to substitute for all these, a universal organization in which all peace-loving nations will finally have a chance
to join.

I am confident that the Congress and the American people
will accept the results of this conference, as the beginnings of a

Roosevelt at Yalta, 1945

permanent structure of peace upon which we can begin to build, under God, that better world in which our children and grand-children—yours and mine, and the children and grandchildren of the whole world—must live, can live. . . .

Papers, 1944–45, 571–572.

The exhausted man with the cadaverous face, showing the approach of death, had finished his work for the nation and for the world.

(36)

JUST as April was beginning Franklin went South to meet the spring. It was his intention to rest and to prepare for the San Francisco meeting. Going to West Georgia when the azaleas bloomed was an old custom, but it was one he had not been able to follow regularly in recent years. Being Commander-in-Chief in wartime had been a confining discipline.

As often as he could, he had used a hideaway camp on Mount Catoctin in nearby Maryland. He had said to reporters who, for security reasons, were asked not to disclose its exact location, that they might call it Shangri-La. This was a reference to the faraway place in James Hilton's popular novel.

Even before the election photographs had shown his exhaustion. There was much concern about his health. Shangri-La was convenient, and the forest surroundings were agreeable; but it was not West Georgia.

There had been changes at Warm Springs. The institution of an annual March of Dimes had yielded funds large enough to establish and support a new and enlarged center for treating the effects of polio. It was a gracious and useful group of buildings and he was proud of it.

Then too the Little White House, now two years old, had had additions to accommodate a few guests and had begun to look as though it really belonged on its hillside among the pines. The farm on Pine Mountain was just about given up; everything Franklin had tried to do there had failed. Only the new plantings of long-leaf pine were prospering. It looked as though the whole ridge ought to be forested—perhaps made into a recreation area. In fact, plans were already being made for what would become the Roosevelt State Park.

In these later years, when Franklin came to visit, it had been with a following of many reporters, secretaries, assistants, and a succession of officials needing his decision on important matters.

Besides the usual Secret Service men who guarded him, because of the war, there were also Marines in new sentry boxes among the pines. It was impressive when the train came in, not much like old arrivals when he had been a hopeful patient.

Soon, however, all the visitors were deployed. The reporters and Secret Service men were put up in Georgia Hall at the Center; the Marines had a camp of their own; and the President was settled in the Little White House. But it was obvious to everyone around him that he was now terribly changed. They recalled the gay and hearty man they had so often looked after, and were sad.

This time he had with him two favorite cousins, quiet, elderly ladies, Laura Delano and Margaret Suckley; and not far away at any time there were William Hassett and Grace Tully, the secretaries who saw to it that he read all the papers and documents Presidents must study and sign. With him too was Lucy Mercer (now Rutherford). She had brought with her a painter to work on what was to be Franklin's last portrait. Their old attachment was still at least a friendship.

The many papers were stacked in neat piles, and as he finished each of them, Hassett spread them wherever he could so that the India ink could dry without being blotted. This gave the room a washday look, and they spoke of the signing sessions as "doing the laundry."

It was pleasant enough on the morning of April 12th. A small fire of fine logs crackled, mockingbirds sang outside, and when the sun had warmed the woods, the doors were opened to the terrace and the resinous smell of the pines came in.

For some days a quiet routine had been followed. But it was obvious that it was not having its usual relaxing effect. Those close to him could no longer ignore a relentless deterioration. He was wasted-looking. His eyes were sunk in dark shadows. And often he sat hunched and silent in the sun or before the fire.

A President always has a doctor to watch his health; and, as Franklin wasted away, an especially close watch was being kept by Dr. Bruenn. Franklin was on an invalid diet prepared with care by Daisy Bonner, the Warm Springs cook who for many years had studied his likes and dislikes. She complained that she could not tempt him now with any of his favorite dishes. This morning he had pushed away his tray and she was in despair.

But he had always especially liked these sharp spring mornings. And on this one he had seemed to work quite cheerfully at "the laundry." The ladies were sitting quietly before the fire. Doctor Bruenn, after looking him over, and finding no cause for immediate alarm, had gone for a swim in the pool. On Franklin's table were not only the many documents he must read, and letters and laws to be signed, but also the draft of the address he expected to make at San Francisco to greet the delegates who, he was now confident, would adopt the charter of the United Nations. The address need only be one of welcome, and of hope for a peaceful world under law.

It was going to be a good day. In the afternoon there was to be a barbecue at the home of an old friend, the Warm Springs mayor, Frank Allcorn, and all the neighbors would be there. They would surround him with friendly attention; no one would mention the great affairs of the Presidency, only the intimate concerns of the village and countryside. And in the evening the patients at the Center, mostly children, were planning a pageant in his honor. He would come home early and be put to bed in his own small room.

Toward noon, Miss Suckley glanced in his direction and gasped to see that his head had fallen to one side and that his hands were lax on the papers before him. She rushed to hold him upright and called out to his big valet, Prettyman. Hassett came too; and while Prettyman lifted the unconscious man in his arms and carried him to his bed, Hassett telephoned frantically for the doctor. There was nothing to be done. It was a massive cerebral hemorrhage. In a few hours he was dead.

Eleanor was in Washington attending a meeting having to do with a charity cause when she was given the message that told her of Franklin's seizure. Soon after getting back to the White House she was told that he had died. She waited for Vice-President Truman to come to her, and when he asked what he could do for her, she asked in return what *she* could do for *him*. For, with very little preparation, he would now have to finish what was in process—a war to be ended, a peace to be made, and a country to be returned to its normal activities.

Then she went by plane down to Atlanta, and to the Springs. During the night, a funeral train drew into the Warm Springs siding readied for carrying the dead President to Washington for services in the East Room of the White House, and then to Hyde Park for burial in the hedged rose garden of Springwood.

It had been a custom, whenever Franklin had been staying at the Little White House, that he would stop in front of Georgia Hall to say good-by. The patients who could would come out, and he would leave in a flurry of cheerful calls. Eleanor arranged that when he was taken to the train in his casket this custom was followed. The hearse and her own car stopped for a few moments where he had so often stopped before. Graham Jackson, who had so often made music at the Calloway gatherings, stood at one side of the group with his accordion. He played "Goin' Home."

When Jackson had finished, the remains of the President were placed on the funeral car. Eleanor described the trip north in the *Ferdinand Magellan*, the car Franklin usually traveled in. His body lay in the *Conneaut*, just behind:

I lay in my berth all night with the window shade up, looking out at the countryside he had loved and watching the faces of the people at the stations, and even at the cross-roads, who came to pay their last tribute all through the night. . . .

I never realized the true scope of the devotion to him until he died. Later I couldn't go into a subway in New York without people stopping me to say they missed the way the President used to talk to them. . . .

There was a real dialogue between Franklin and the people. . . .

After the White House ceremonies in the East Room, and, after he had been carried up Pennsylvania Avenue to the station, the train took him north again to the small station down by the river at Hyde Park. His body, on a caisson, was drawn up the road through the woods to the burial place. The Episcopal service was read by the venerable rector of the St. James Chapel where Franklin had been a member all his life. Taps were blown, a salute fired. His Scottie dog Fala barked furiously.

It was over. Eleanor stayed after the crowd had gone away. Then she too followed the rest out the driveway to the Post Road and to her cottage at the back of the estate. She would now go on with the work she had given herself to do, no longer a President's wife, but a strong force just the same.

As the coffin was lowered, the rector spoke the lines of John Ellerton:

> Now the laborer's task is o'er;
>   Now the battle day is past;
> Now upon the farther shore
>   Lands the voyager at last.
>   Father, in thy gracious keeping
>   Leave we now Thy servant sleeping.

Postscript

ELEANOR lived on until 1962. She continued to be very busy. Until Eisenhower became President and dismissed her, she was a United States delegate to the United Nations; she wrote a widely read newspaper column and another for a monthly magazine; she entertained many visiting notables at the cottage where the family had so often picnicked beside the swimming pool; she made innumerable speeches before many different groups and was unfailingly helpful to people who sought her out.

When she fell ill, the whole world was concerned, and when she died, she was mourned as few women ever have been.

She lies beside her husband now in the high-hedged rose garden at Springwood. It was where Franklin had based himself as he launched his political career. And Eleanor had become familiar with it as a wife whose children had known it as home. It was fitting that they should be together there.

Before he died Franklin had willed Springwood to the nation and arranged for the building of a nearby museum and library. It was planned with characteristic care to harmonize with the Dutch Colonial style of the Hudson Valley. In it he had deposited all his papers and mementos; and the visitor will find there vast accumulations from his years in public life.

Franklin also planned the ceremony of his passing and the kind of marker to be put on his grave. He had avoided pretension. The funeral was to be low-keyed. The stone was to be plain, and the inscription spare.

So the visitor sees it now. As he directed, no eulogy elaborates the two names. Only the dates show the span of their lives. This simplicity is a reminder of the democracy and equality it symbolizes. The life-work of the two who lie there was the establishment of the freedoms they spoke of so eloquently.

It had been subtle political craftsmanship, suitable to the particular institutions of the United States that enabled Franklin in a measure to prevail. But the ends were as plain as the marker and as solid.

The words left off the gravestone are more eloquent than any that could have been put there. America was a nation sounder and stronger because the Roosevelts had been its mentors for a time. Americans were more democratic, more equal, because the Roosevelts had helped shape their minds. If their well-being was increased, so also was their sense of neighborly duty. Franklin himself put America's progress like this:

> Ours has been a story of vigorous challenges which have been accepted and overcome—challenges of uncharted seas, of wild forests and desert plains, of raging floods and withering droughts, of foreign tyrants and domestic strife, of staggering problems—social, economic, and physical; and we have come out of them the most powerful Nation—and the freest—in all history.

Papers, 1941, 444.

If we hope to understand these leaders in their time it has constantly to be recalled that they lived through a technological revolution and that they led in the nation's accommodation to it. Telephones, electric lights, radio, and television, even the internal combustion engine—to say nothing of the new and strange nuclear sources of power—were all in the future when they were young.

Their particular circumstances have an antique cast as we regard them now. They belonged to old and firmly rooted families, wealthy, surrounded by servants, and feeling themselves entitled by birth to privileges common people did not have. Until they were grown neither had reason to recognize how unfair it was that their good fortune was not shared by others. They did come to understand, however, that inequality was intolerable, and that democracy was not only the fairest kind of political arrangement, but probably inevitable as well. Here is Roosevelt speaking on the subject in Gainesville, Georgia, 1938:

> . . . the continuation of the American system calls for the elimination of special privilege, the dissemination of the whole of the truth, and participation in prosperity by the people at the bottom of the ladder, as well as those in the middle and at the top.

Once Franklin and Eleanor Roosevelt saw their duty, they devoted themselves with ardor and skill to seeing that all human kind were benefited by the wonderful machinery of modern industry. They were in the full tradition of our democracy, a tradition returned to after a period when it seemed in danger of dying. They not only "overcame" their aristocratic upbringing, they made it easier for all to follow in the way they went. On democracy, Roosevelt said this in North Carolina, 1938:

> My anchor is democracy—and more democracy. And, my friends, I am of the firm belief that the nation by an overwhelming majority, supports my opposition to vesting supreme power in the hands of any class, numerous, but select.

Franklin will always be admired because he succeeded in spite of so many reasons why he could have failed. Americans recall that he had been slow in maturing; that he was wealthy and had no need to work for a living; and that, although he had survived one of the most terrible of all diseases, it had left him a hopeless cripple. They understand that in the struggle for recovery he had had to learn hard lessons of patience and persistence. His was a hard and demanding

262

career, always just within his strength. And it is marvelous to remember how gaily he undertook it, and with what light-heartedness he accepted the discipline that he could never relax.

Eleanor's ordeal had not been much easier. Because she was an orphan, her vast capacity for love and service had always been thwarted until she found a husband and had a family of her own. It was only when the children were grown, and her husband on the way to becoming famous, that she had discovered the friendless and underprivileged whose condition she could help to improve.

There exists a great interest among Americans—and, for that matter, among other people—about this thirty-second President. It is an interest which grows rather than declines. Along with the simple sorrow of those who lent themselves to his leadership, who trusted him to be their better selves and gain their better ends, there prevails a much more sophisticated interest. Its center is the place prepared by the President himself at Hyde Park. There are gathered not only the mementos of his personal life, the ice boat he used on the Hudson, the choiserie from his desk, his various extraordinary collections, even his favorite furniture —but also the mountains of paper out of which, sifted and compared and analyzed, political historians will try to learn something of how a man gets to be President and how he manages the Presidency. This last, no less than the uncritical reverence of ordinary folk, will go on and on. It will not develop any certainties, perhaps not even much wisdom, for future statesmen. It has begun to dispel some myths which could be of no service to a great man's memory—such, for instance, as that of a kind of infallibility, which some of his uncritical followers would perpetuate if they could.

What is emerging from this just-beginning analysis is the portrait of a man who maneuvered endlessly for political preferment, learned his trade in professional fashion, rose to the greatest office in America, and then had to struggle just as endlessly, with the means he had and understood, to gain for his people the ends he saw as imperative to their future. The struggle was a political one; it was neither clean nor pretty. His opponents were unscrupulous, powerful, and determined. He had to gain his people's victories against odds, often, and always against potentially powerful opposition. They—the people—judged that he succeeded. The methods he used they were not aware of; mostly they were not interested. He had no support for niceness and scrupulosity; if he adhered to such standards it was because another course offended something inside himself, not because he feared any disapproval. He had those scruples. They came from his parents, his school, his church. But all his experience taught him that they had to be compromised in politics. Fire had to be fought with fire. When he died he had been through perhaps the most sublime ordeal of contemporary humanity. If he could speak to those who remain behind him, he would be the last to gloss over the trials he underwent, to belittle the baseness of the struggles he often had to carry on, or to claim that his ends were not more noble than his means. He would say that perhaps he had been mistaken, but that with what he had at the time, he had done his best.

"The Compromising Roosevelt," *Western Political Quarterly,* VI, 41.

The symbolism of the plain stone in the Springwood garden, then, is clear enough. We are to make our own inscription. We are to recall the Roosevelts for their leadership, for the well-being they helped Americans to reach, and for the democracy they asked the world to practice—as it was practiced by themselves.

Some Additional Readings

Allen, F. L. *Since Yesterday*. New York: Harper & Row, Publishers, 1940.

Burns, J. M. *Roosevelt: The Lion and the Fox*. New York: Harcourt, Brace, & World, Inc., 1956.

Byrnes, J. F. *Speaking Frankly*. New York: Harper & Row, Publishers, 1947.

Churchill, Winston S. *The Second World War*. 6 vols. Boston: Houghton Mifflin Company, 1948–53.

Daniels, Jonathan. *The End of Innocence*. Philadelphia: J. B. Lippincott Company, 1954.

———. *The Years Between the Wars*. New York: Doubleday & Company, Inc., 1966.

Eisenhower, D. D. *Crusade in Europe*. New York: Doubleday & Company, Inc., 1948.

Freidel, Frank. *Franklin D. Roosevelt*. 6 vols. Boston: Little, Brown and Company, 1950, 1954, 1956, etc.

Gunther, John. *Roosevelt in Retrospect*. New York: Harper & Row, Publishers, 1950.

Lorant, Stefan. *FDR: A Pictorial Biography*. New York: Simon and Schuster, Inc., 1950.

Nesbitt, Henrietta. *White House Diary*. New York: Doubleday & Company, Inc., 1948.

Nevins, Allan. *The New Deal and World Affairs, 1933–1945*. New Haven: Yale University Press, 1950.

Perkins, Frances. *The Roosevelt I Knew*. New York: The Viking Press, 1946.

The Public Papers and Addresses of Franklin D. Roosevelt. 13 vols. Compiled by Samuel I. Rosenman, with Notes and Introduction by Franklin D. Roosevelt. New York: Random House, Inc., 5 vols., 1938; The Macmillan Company, 4 vols., 1941; Harper & Row, Publishers, 4 vols., 1950.

Roosevelt, Eleanor. *This I Remember*. New York: Harper & Row, Publishers, 1949.

———. *This Is My Story*. New York: Harper & Row, Publishers, 1937.

Roosevelt, Elliott, ed. *F. D. R.: His Personal Letters*. 4 vols. New York: Duell, Sloan & Pearce, Inc., 1947.

Rosenman, Samuel I. *Working With Roosevelt*. New York: Harper & Row, Publishers, 1952.

Rossiter, Clinton. *The American Presidency*. New York: Harcourt, Brace & World, Inc., 1956.

Schlesinger, A. M. *The Crisis of the Old Order*. Boston: Houghton Mifflin Company, 1957.

Sherwood, Robert E. *Roosevelt and Hopkins*. New York: Harper & Row, Publishers, 1948.

Stiles, Lela. *The Man Behind Roosevelt: The Story of Louis McHenry Howe*. New York: The World Publishing Company, 1954.

Walker, Turnley. *Roosevelt and the Warm Springs Story*. New York: A. A. Wyn, Inc., Publishers, 1953.

Wecter, Dixon. *The Age of the Great Depression, 1929–41*. New York: The Macmillan Company, 1948.

Index